Rocks and Wildlife Around the Axe

Donald Campbell

Dear Sarah

Not as big as 'your' bird book and plenty of colour to share with James, Ollie and Charlie.

Big D

Feb 2020

Axe Vale & District Conservation Society
AV&DCS

First published in 2020 and © by Axe Vale & District Conservation Society

Ruth Gray, Treasurer and Membership Secretary of AVDCS
www.axevaleconservation.org.uk

Text © Donald Campbell 2020

ISBN 978-1-9162819-0-5

The right of Donald Campbell to be identified as the author of this work has been asserted in accordance with the Copyright, Designs and Patents Act 1988, sections 77 and 78.

No part of this publication may be reproduced, stored in a retrieval system or transmitted in any form or by any means without the prior permission of the publisher and copyright owner.

This book is sold subject to the condition that all designs are copyright and are not for commercial reproduction without the permission of the designer and copyright owner.

Photographs and other images are credited where they appear. All unmarked photographs were taken by the author. Whilst every effort has been made to obtain permission from the copyright holders for all material used in this book, the publishers will be pleased to hear from anyone who has not been appropriately acknowledged, and to make a correction in future reprints.

Designer & Editor: John Marriage

Printed in England by AB Print

Also by Donald Campbell

The Encyclopedia of British Birds (1999)
A Dempsey Parr book for Paragon, 384pp.

Exploring the Undercliffs (2006)
Coastal Publishing, for the Jurassic Coast Trust and English Nature, 64pp.

Rocks and Wildlife Around the Axe

Donald Campbell

Spoonbill - a rare visitor to the estuary

Rock at the east end of the Chasm

Wonderful wildlife and spectacular locations

"The ninety five miles of the Dorset and East Devon Coast ranks as one of the world's most precious natural sites. I really cannot express how grateful I am to all who take part in efforts to protect one of the country's greatest treasures." – Prince Charles, sending 'warmest congratulations' on the tenth anniversary of the nomination of the World Heritage Site, 2011.

"The World Heritage Site is an extremely prestigious but well-earned distinction of the Jurassic Coast. It is indeed of worldwide importance and a place of great fascination to anyone interested in the history of life on this planet. Let us hope on this, the tenth anniversary of its granting, we do our best not only to maintain but to improve the ways by which we enable visitors to understand its significance." – Sir David Attenborough, on behalf of '10 years: Dorset and East Devon World Heritage Site' (2011).

"Natural Seaton: celebrating the natural heritage of the Seaton area – particularly as a gateway to the Jurassic Coast World Heritage site – and, through engaging the local community and visitors to the town, developing long-lasting support for its conservation." - Doug Hulyer, on behalf of the Natural Seaton Partnership, 2011.

This book is dedicated to Nicky who, despite illness has remained caring to all, even when unable to garden or read.

Rocks and Wildlife Around the Axe

Contents

3-12   Geology and Landscape: Seaton's great location and the World Heritage Coast

13-24 History of the valley: Travellers, geologists and continual change

25-35 Conservation initiatives: Threats and solutions on land and at sea

36-49 The estuary and its wildlife: Mainly birds, but they are only part of estuary life

50-60 West to Beer and out to sea: White cliffs, soft cliffs and changing attitudes to marine life

61-71 East into the Undercliffs: Ongoing change as the Undercliffs NNR is established and managed

72-73 Recent developments and the perspective of time

74-88 References, explanations, acknowledgements and index

Introductory words: Doug Hulyer

Doug, as Trustee and former Chair of the Jurassic Coast Trust and long-term supporter of Seaton Jurassic, has done much to promote the attractions of the Dorset and East Devon coast.

"It was on an A-level zoology field course at the end of the 1960s that Seaton revealed its wonders to me – the web of life and the tree of life in all their glory – and set me on a lifetime course dedicated to nature conservation. Places speak to people, but every now and then their deeper stories are hidden from view. This is where the Interpretation or Discovery Centre, the skilled guide or mentor, or the inspirational author can all make their mark. All those years ago it was the skills and enthusiasm of my A-level tutor that made the difference for me.

Today we have the Seaton Jurassic Centre and many organisations that support the Seaton initiative to guide the curious, whether they are young or old. As President of the Axe Vale and District Conservation Society, as a Trustee of Seaton Visitor Centre and through his deep involvement in the East Devon Area of Outstanding Natural Beauty, Seaton Wetlands, Holyford Woods and the Undercliff, Donald Campbell has been a leading light for both. This book is a great introduction to the natural secrets of the area and I hope will inspire everyone to get out and discover the wonders for themselves."

GEOLOGY AND LANDSCAPE

Passengers on flight BE1534 from Amsterdam to Exeter on 17 October 2009 had been able to see little below them until views of Chichester harbour, the Solent and the Isle of Wight suddenly appeared as clouds parted. Soon the Chalk of Old Harry Rocks indicated the start of the Dorset

Lighthouse at Portland

and East Devon World Heritage Coast and the peninsulas of Purbeck and Portland, with Lulworth Cove and Durdle Door between, were clear below. After that there was only the sea until the plane turned inland over the Undercliff where Natural England and their volunteers had recently been mowing and raking off the cut vegetation to reduce fertility on flower rich grassland. West of Seaton the white Chalk of Beer Head contrasted with the red Triassic cliffs extending towards Sidmouth and beyond. These, like so much of the coast have long been subject to landslips, as William Stukeley observed in 1723 "The waves perpetually undermine the strata of stone which from time to time fall down in great parcels".

As the plane flew over the Axe estuary there were views of the recently created and flooded Black Hole Marsh, its islands and the saltmarsh of Colyford Common. More height was lost over Colyton as the flight approached Exeter, giving ever closer views of the mosaic of fields, woods and hedges so characteristic of the East Devon Area of Outstanding Natural Beauty.

In about a minute we had flown across the area to be described in this book which is much the same as that covered in the Axe Estuary and Seaton Bay Bird Reports which included records from within 5 km of Axmouth Bridge. The area described is also the centre of the activities of the Axe Vale and District Conservation Society.

The East Devon Way crosses the north of this part of the Area of Outstanding Natural Beauty with walkers going along the rivers Coly and Axe and on to Musbury, before climbing to the Iron Age hillfort with great views across the Axe and along the coast to Beer. The route continues on field paths and quiet roads to the river Lym and Lyme Regis.

Beer Head and Stormy Waters

HENRY JAGGERS

A FLIGHT ALONG THE COAST

GEOLOGY AND LANDSCAPE

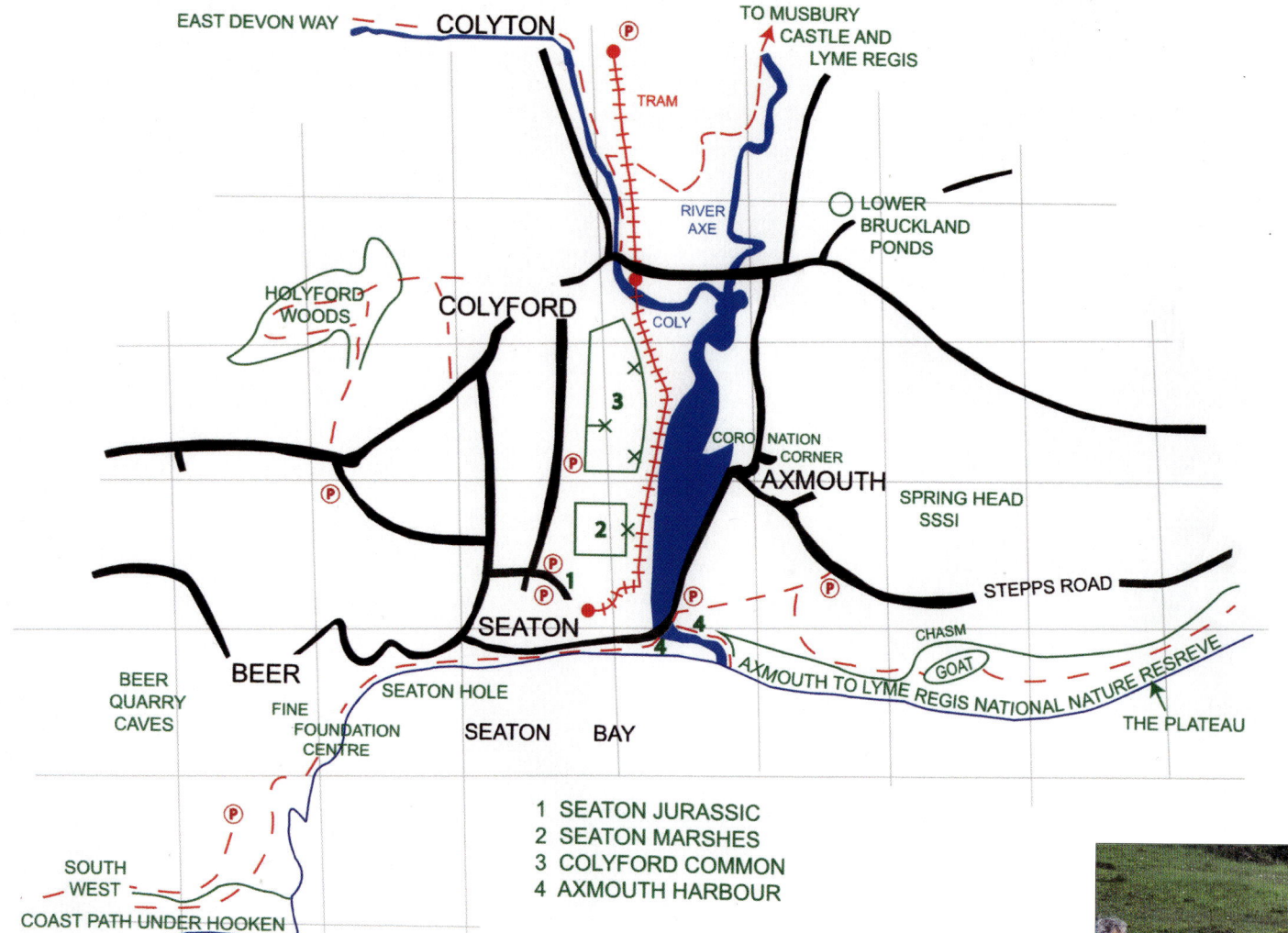

MAP OF THE AREA

- 1 SEATON JURASSIC
- 2 SEATON MARSHES
- 3 COLYFORD COMMON
- 4 AXMOUTH HARBOUR

Colin Pady and Mark Williams at Horriford Farm for the opening of the Holyford Woods LNR

Stedcombe from the Axe

A picnic on Goat Island

GEOLOGY AND LANDSCAPE 5

A GEOLOGICAL MAP

Over the Plateau

Geology around the Axe

ALLUVIUM ALONG THE RIVERS

COLY
AXE
COLYFORD
AXMOUTH
Rousdon
SEATON
BEER
UNDERCLIFFS
SEATON BAY
BEER HEAD

- CLAY WITH FLINTS
- UPPER GREENSAND AND CHALK
- TRIASSIC MUDSTONE

From Goat Island to Charton Bay in the Undercliffs

UK PERSPECTIVES

GEOLOGY AND LANDSCAPE

THE UNDERLYING GEOLOGY

West of Lyme Regis the Sidmouth road leads to Rousdon, set on a level platform shown brown on sheet 326 of the British Geological Survey maps. Brown represents clay-with-flints which Edwards and Gallois, in an explanation of the sheet, describe as forming "a gently undulating plateau that caps all the high ground in the Sidmouth District."

The clay-with-flints has a complex origin involving different processes acting on a variety of sediments and rocks over a long period of time. Where the Chalk and Greensand has been dissolved or eroded away, insoluble sheets of flint and chert gravel are left, along with sands and clays.

Down the hill towards the Axe the map shows bands of green, indicating Upper Greensand and Chalk before, on lower ground towards Boshill Cross, an orangey brown represents the Triassic Branscombe Mudstone. From Boshill, across the valley bottom, pale yellow on the map indicates the Axe alluvium which "can be divided into two areas, the meander belt of the present day river, in which sedimentation occurs in times of flood, and a slightly higher outer zone in which sedimentation has virtually ceased."

Colyford is on the Branscombe Mudstone, often overlain by quaternary gravels and clays. Well up the steep western side of the valley Greensand briefly reappears before the road, heading for Sidmouth, is back on another plateau with clay-with-flints. Dotted lines on the map, representing faults, cross the road near the old Seaton water tower, now a private house. These faults are fractures caused by past earthquakes; they are more obvious on the coast east of Beer.

The Axe and Coly with a developing oxbow lake

The gently undulating plateau seen from Colyton Community Woodland

BEN OSBORNE

> While walking from London to Penzance in 1892 Charles Harper described how, for three hours, "there and back" train travellers from London "... snatched a fearful joy. At other times Seaton is sluggish and dull and the bourgeois plastered buildings are an insult to the magnificent scenery on either hand."

This scenery, with the Cretaceous and Triassic rocks of Haven Cliff on the one hand and the spectacular Chalk and sandstone formations of Seaton Hole and Whitecliff on the other, give the town its very special setting. The higher western cliffs contrast with the lower late Triassic ones near the town and with the lower parts of Haven Cliff to the east. Two miles further east fossil rich Jurassic limestone slabs are well exposed on the beach so that rocks characteristic of each of the three periods of the Mesozoic can be reached on foot from Seaton. Nearer to the town than the "slabs", but less accessible, is the mile long chasm which formed overnight in the landslip of 1839, isolating a Chalk mass, now known as Goat Island, from the arable fields inland.

Triassic rocks at the base of Haven Cliff formed in equatorial deserts

The mouth of the Axe from Haven Cliff before recent developments

GEOLOGY AND LANDSCAPE

THE COAST BECOMES A WORLD HERITAGE SITE

BEN OSBORNE

On 13 December 2001 the undeveloped cliffs and beaches between Studland, near Poole in Dorset, and Orcombe Point, near Exmouth in East Devon were "inscribed on the World Heritage list" by UNESCO, the United Nations education and science organisation. Seaton became one of the eight man-made frontages or Gateway Towns which are not part of the Heritage site. "What makes the concept of World Heritage exceptional is its universal application. World Heritage Sites belong to all peoples of the world irrespective of the territory on which they are located". The implication of being on the World Heritage list is that properties have outstanding universal value and a "cultural and/or natural significance which is so exceptional as to transcend national boundaries and to be of common importance to present and future generations of all humanity".

The site was granted its status under UNESCO's criterion eight – earth history and geological features including rocks, representing 185 million years, important fossil localities, as at Charmouth and Lyme Regis, and textbook geomorphological features as at Ladram Bay and Chesil Beach.

In 2017 the Jurassic Coast Trust and its Partnership Advisory Committee (PAC) took over management of the coast as county council budgets continued to fall. In February 2019 the PAC agreed on a set of values to protect the coast for future generations as set out in the 2020-25 Partnership Plan. This comments that the sometimes controversial idea, that coastal conservation is underpinned by ongoing erosion, is key to conservation of the site.

> 'The coastline only exists because of erosion and over time this has exposed world class geology and palaeontology, and created iconic landforms that so many people know and love.'

Lulworth Cove

Left - Chesil Beach and the Fleet

SAM ROSE

GEOLOGY AND LANDSCAPE

Seaton Seafront

On 10 July 2002 *Pulman's Weekly News* had the headline "Unique resort could become an eco-tourism destination" above its report on a discussion paper produced by Seaton Development Trust. Since that time, land to the west of the tramline has become wetter, more accessible and better for both wildlife and people, as East Devon Countryside Service has developed the Seaton Wetlands.

While the wetlands were developing there were constant difficulties with plans for some sort of Interpretation Centre in Seaton, until Doug Hulyer, with wide experience in developing the Wildfowl Trust at Slimbridge and the London Wetland Centre, was invited to act as consultant.

Doug had first come to Devon as an A-level student looking at and into rock pools at Seaton Hole. He loved the shore below Whitecliff and had repeatedly returned. In a report *Delivering a Vision, Encouraging Regeneration*, he emphasised that for over a decade a vision for the town's natural heritage had developed within the community and that, in his words, the vision was "The desire to create a permanent centre that celebrates through creative and highly enjoyable discovery, exhibits and events, the natural wealth of the area. Linked information and interpretation at key locations, Axmouth Harbour, the Axe Wetlands, Seaton Hole, the Undercliffs and at the town's seafront will become exciting 'minihubs' or natural Seaton 'hot spots' on a Seaton Explorer Trail." In 2012 Devon Wildlife Trust was the preferred bidder following interviews with those expressing an interest in establishing the potential centre.

As always money was critical but in 2014, following detailed planning, a grant of £300,000 was awarded by the Coastal Communities Fund for the renamed Seaton Jurassic project. Later in the year Pulman's *View From* had the headline "Jurassic Centre is on!" as Councillor Ian Thomas told of a £620,000 Heritage Lottery grant while the Fine Family Foundation made yet another donation to a coastal centre. The Jurassic Coast Trust, now with Doug Hulyer as chairman, won another Lottery award enabling it to appoint a community project officer to raise money to safeguard the World Heritage Site and support the Jurassic Coast Partnership.

On 26 September 2014 a groundbreaking ceremony signalled the start of the building with East Devon District Council as a principal financial supporter, working with the Devon Wildlife Trust as centre operator and part funder. Plans for the learning experience and exhibition space were led by Helen Shackleton and Lloyd Turner with support from DWT's Steve Hussey.

Seaton Primary School pupils help the author to 'break the ground'

GEOLOGY AND LANDSCAPE

Looking east from the clifftop near Beer Head

GEOLOGY AND LANDSCAPE

LOOKING EAST FROM BEER HEAD

The spectacular Chalk at Beer Head could be said to be in the wrong place. It was brought down to sea level by the fault that runs north from Seaton Hole and is much younger than the red Triassic mudstone to the east. This obscures the message of a "Walk through Time" when rocks are said to be consistently younger as one moves east along the Jurassic Coast from Exmouth. As well as faults and landslips, synclines and anticlines also obscure the general message which is dependent on the gentle dip of most rock strata towards the east.

From the gun battery, dating from the Napoleonic wars, the left hand side of the view is dominated by Chalk at the top of Whitecliff with Annis' Knob visible above the shrubs. Different layers in the knob appear again in the cliffs at Dowlands and Pinhay, and can be correlated with similar beds in Sussex and Northern France. In the middle, towards Seaton and beyond the major fault at Seaton Hole, are low Mercia Mudstone cliffs with the green Axmouth hills beyond the town to the right.

A long, geologically recent pebble bank separates Seaton from the waters of Lyme Bay. The bank's development has forced the Axe eastwards so that it now reaches the sea under Haven Cliff. Further east the lower parts of this cliff change colour from red, to pink and greyish green, but all the rock is of Triassic origin formed under desert conditions near the Equator. The varying availability of water and oxygen in the remote past account for the colour changes.

Apart from the conspicuous Chalk, the higher parts of Haven Cliff provide one of the best sections of the Greensand in Britain. These Cretaceous rocks are 'in situ' but rocks of similar age at Culverhole Point are 'ex situ' as a mass, showing that almost the whole of the Upper Greensand has slipped down to the beach but remained intact. Bindon Sandstone can be seen below the Chalk and above the Whitecliff Chert. Further east are the most westerly Jurassic rocks, sloping slabs of Blue Lias. Many of the fine fossils have recently been buried during storms but the slabs still make a fine picnic spot.

Chalk and Upper Greensand above the scrub of Haven Cliff

The slipped mass in Culverhole sea-cliff

> "The whole surface of the land is exposed to the chemical action of the air and the rainwater with its carbonic acid and, in colder countries to frost; the disintegrated matter is carried down even gentle slopes during heavy rain ... and it is then transported by streams and rivers which, when rapid, deepen the channels and triturate the fragments". (Charles Darwin, *Origin of Species*, sixth edition (1902) p.417.)

Pioneering geologist William Buckland could not believe that the depth of the Axe Valley, whose steep sides have been mentioned, could be explained by the long acting forces of erosion currently operating. Instead he felt, with the orthodox Christian beliefs of the time, that it was evidence of a comparatively recent Noah's flood as described in his *Reliquiae Diluvianae* of 1823 or the previous year's *Excavations of valleys which intersect the south coast of Devon and Dorset*. As a catastrophist he believed in the efficacy of occasional violent events in shaping landscapes. By contrast uniformitarians believe that the processes acting today create, over vast periods of time, the cliffs and valleys which now exist so that the landslip that led to the Undercliff at Beer is seen as a violent but normal event.

Hooken Undercliff and pinnacles at Beer

Sir Charles Lyell, geological mentor of Charles Darwin, was an early uniformitarian and as such knew that immense periods of time must have been involved in creating present day landscapes. One of the ways that Darwin tried to visualise time was to consider the gradual denudation of the dome over the Weald. Between the Chalk escarpment of the North Downs and the sandy Hastings Beds exposed in Ashdown Forest in the corner of the Wealden dome, some 600m have been eroded since it was forced up as a result of pressure from the Alpine earth movement some 15 million years ago. Strata, originally in flat sheets, were uplifted and then gradually eroded leaving the relatively hard Chalk to form the Downs.

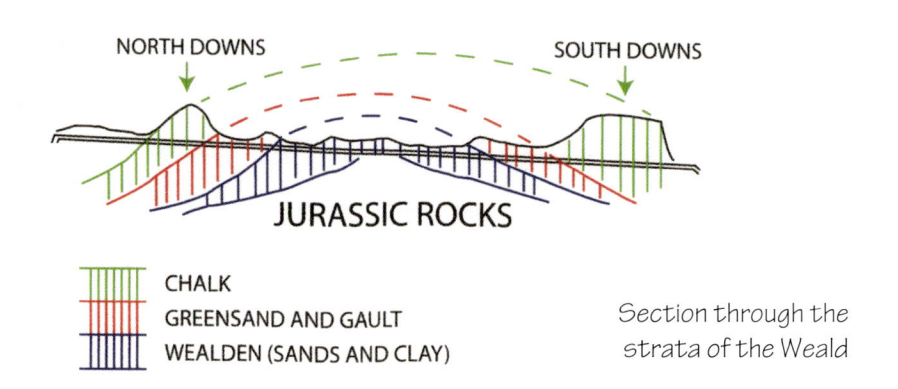

In the discussion paper prepared by Seaton Development Trust in 2002 Ramues Gallois, writing about local geology and geomorphology, the study of processes which shape landscape, describe the Axe as being "One of the best examples of a "misfit" river valley in southern England, with its great width having been carved out by ice-sheet meltwater around 10,000 years ago."

Section through the strata of the Weald

The five fields abutting the tramline would become Black Hole Marsh

HISTORY OF THE VALLEY

In an attempt to find out more of the ecological history of these 10,000 years a team from the University of Winchester carried out a bioarchaeological survey in April 2008. They took samples of sediment from 31 boreholes along 5 transects while larger samples were taken from special boreholes, 41 and 42, using powerful pneumatic hammers; these 1000 mm long samples were later analysed in the laboratory. Other boreholes used hand operated equipment, with sediments retained in the head of the auger and studied in the field.

The samples from borehole 42 at the western edge of Seaton Marshes and transects 1 and 2 suggested periodic incursions of the sea in the southern kilometre. Radiocarbon dating suggested that the base of this long core was some 4500 years old with the upper levels about 1500 years before present. The core from borehole 41 in the middle of transect 3, contained wood peat with alder pollen. Above it was swamp peat, characterised by sedge pollen and fern spores. Between the peat layers pollen of Sea Blite and Sea Plantain suggested a time of sea level rise. Presence of diatom species, adapted to different salinities, indicated freshwater, brackish or marine habitats.

Higher upriver it seems that at the end of the Neolithic, the estuary, south of present day Colyford Common, would have been a complex of saltmarshes separated by tidal creeks or freshwater fen.

At the opening of Colyford Common LNR

Later, after the Bronze and Iron ages, sea level rise led to the formation of a bay, Axe Haven, with relatively deep water extending towards today's Black Hole Marsh. Saltmarsh may have continued to the north with alder again along the valley edges. There was pasture and cultivated land on surrounding slopes.

A relative fall in estuary level in mediaeval times, perhaps linked with the eastward movement of the pebble bank across the mouth of the river led to the return of saltmarsh with mudflats and creeks near the mouth and vegetated saltmarsh to the north.

Samples from transect 4 on either side of the Stafford Brook suggest that the area has been upper saltmarsh for most of its history. Transect 5 which doglegged across the Coly and northern fields revealed freshwater deposits alternating with those from intertidal processes. The fact that Mesolithic finds were all near the surface suggests that silt deposition was limited. The comparatively recent phase of land reclamation began in the 17th century.

Mudflats near the mouth of the Axe

Whatever the uncertainties linked with this brief study, there is no doubt that children much enjoyed the slushy mud that they extracted from their augurs as they replicated the sampling technique and saw the layers of different coloured sediment taken from different depths.

'Replicating the technique'

The Haven must have reached up to Axmouth or even as far as Stedcombe, "The landing place near the valley", when the Danes raided between 850 and 950 A.D. and when Athelstan, king of the Mercians and West Saxons, invaded in the 10th century. In 1086, twenty years after the successful Norman invasion, the Domesday survey referred to Seaton as Flueta. The Saxon estate 'Aet Fleote' probably included Seaton and Beer when it was granted by King Ethelred to the noble thane Eadsize in 1005.

In 2005 Colin Pady led a walk down the double hedge from his Horriford farm and along the Stafford Brook to celebrate 1000 years of this boundary between Seaton and Colyton. A repeat of this walk in 2010, after Bluebell Day in the woods, had a different symbolism, suggesting the way the Stafford Brook links the contrasting local nature reserves of Holyford Woods and Colyford Common.

'Aet Fleote' was soon divided and in 1086 both Fleote and Bera belonged to Horton Abbey. By 1122 they had both passed to Sherborne Abbey when a bull of Eugenius III confirmed a vast roll of possessions to the Abbot of Sherborne including the settlements of Fleote, Beer and Seaton, the first appearance of that name, with the existing salt pans and other appurtenances.

The present church of St Gregory dates from the early 14th century. A little later Seaton was regarded as a significant port, but after the great storm of 1377 and the silting up of the estuary there was such a deterioration that Bishop Lacey of Exeter granted forty days of indulgence to those contributing to the work "on a new harbour on the seashore at Seaton".

The Rev. John Swete drew St Gregory's, with Axmouth behind, on 20th February 1795

The pebble bank that led to the silting up of the estuary and the site of recent developments on ancient marshland

HISTORY OF THE VALLEY

VISITORS TO SEATON 1723-1865

In 1577, after the dissolution of the monasteries, Seaton Manor was acquired by the Willoughby family. 100 years later, John, the great-great-grandson of the original purchaser, set about reclaiming Seaton Marshes which had only been waste or rough grazing. His project, described by Margaret Parkinson in 1985, involved the building of a bank, on which the trams now run, to separate the estuary and freshwater marshes. His daughter Mary married George Trevelyan and when John died in 1682 his estates passed to that family. The Trevelyans became interested in salt production when the 1702-1712 war with France made the import of salt difficult. Four Trevelyan salt pans were sketched by William Stukely when he visited Seaton in 1723. He also included a watchtower at the mouth of the Axe, the Barrow which he describes as "a ruined square, brick pharos upon a little eminence. They remember it as being 16 foot high and two guns lie there". This eminence was probably originally a small island but as shingle moved east to form a bar, the river mouth was also pushed east.

Another visitor, the Rev. John Swete who arrived from Lyme Regis on 20th February 1795, believed that Seaton would rise to celebrity "by progressive advancement to elegance and expense though it has but little expanse of beach and that bad, yet between high Mountainous hills it has a sheltered situation and the environments in point of picturesque beauty and varied rides are equal if not superior to most of the coast."

Swete's *Travels in Georgian Devon* was published by Devon Books in 1998 and in 2000 they produced Peter Orlando Hutchinson's *Travels in Victorian Devon*. Hutchinson was well-known for his watercolour sketches of Sidmouth and district. His illustrated account of the great landslip was published in 1840 in the Penny Magazine.

It was only in 1865, after a visit to Hawkesdown hillfort and Axmouth Church that he came to Honey Ditches but as he says "it is an earthwork only recently known to us". Tiles more than an inch thick were amongst the rubbish, and fragments of powdered brick which had been mixed with mortar, an indication of Roman work.

View of 'The Landslip' looking west, January 14th 1840 (Hutchinson)

View of 'The Landslip' looking east, January 14th 1840 (Hutchinson)

Moridunum Aug 20 1723

HISTORY OF THE VALLEY

Swete painted the quarry on 23rd February 1795

Nowhere locally is there a greater sense of history than at Beer Quarry Caves where the Romans were the first to extract the special stone. John Scott and Gladys Gray maintain, in *Out of Darkness* (2004), that most people pay tribute to the men who fashioned cathedrals and castles but that few "have given even a passing thought to the men who provided them with their raw material by working deep underground enduring conditions of extreme hardship and danger to wrest the stone from its natural bed."

Unquarried columns support the roof

Quarrymen laboured at the caves for some 2000 years with their strength, together with that of horse and ox, the only power used in creating the enormous complex that now exists.

Although it is apparent that the Romans extracted vast amounts of stone the only authenticated finding of its use in their buildings is in the Honey Ditches villa at Seaton. When the bath house was excavated in 1969 the quoins of the hot room walls, the filas that supported the floors and the flue linings were all proved to be of Beer stone.

The magnificent cross in Colyton church shows that the Saxons used the stone but it was the arrival of the Normans, with improved technology and the urge to build on a grand scale, that revitalised the quarry. The stone, cream-coloured, smooth textured limestone, is unique in its soft texture when fresh, which allowed masons to carve quickly and in fine detail before the stone rapidly hardened.

Side galleries allowed the quarrymen to work on several faces at the same time. Massive unquarried columns were left to support the roof. Exeter Cathedral drew heavily on the stone from the 11th century while further afield it was used in Westminster Hall and Abbey, for the capping stones of London Bridge and in Winchester Cathedral.

It was thought that the Tower of London, built in 1086, used only stone from Caen but the White Tower does include 4-ton blocks from Beer.

The Great Screen in Winchester Cathedral carved from Beer Stone

EXTRACTING AND TRANSPORTING STONE

Workers used only primitive hand tools and generations of them daily faced up to blank walls of rock, into which they had to pick and hack their way. Black powder, an attendant new danger, came in the middle of the 16th century but it was soon found to fracture stone, so it was back to pickaxes. All the work, whether done precariously balanced on makeshift platforms or crouching to wield the pick, was carried out in darkness relieved only by the feeble lights of tallow candles. Accurately cut blocks, usually four foot cubes, were eventually removed after wedges had been inserted to help extricate the stone. The quality of the block was assessed and if its value was reduced by irregularities the wages of the quarrymen were appropriately reduced.

Barges from the beach were one vital form of transport but horses were essential and Exeter Cathedral had wheeled carts from the end of the 13th century. Horse-drawn wagons could take stone as far as Lincoln or York.

Until the 17th century oxen were the powerhouses for taking heavy loads uphill with a 'truckamuck' of four small trees making a crude sledge. At least transport had improved when, in 1909, hundreds of tonnes were shipped to New York and then taken 1000 miles overland for use in Christchurch Cathedral, St Louis, Missouri.

Greater Horseshoe Bats are among the seven species which hibernate in the caves. They cluster to keep warm, and perhaps to reduce water loss, while, unlike other bats, they wrap their wings around their bodies.

In 2008 Pete Youngman of the East Devon AONB team initiated a three year 'looking out for bats' project to find out more about their movements and their breeding and feeding activities. They may fly up to 10 km in a night in search of moths and beetles with dung beetles being a particular favourite in late summer. The Beer bats are now being studied by Dr Fiona Matthews who featured, with the bats and Quarry Caves, in TVs *Countryfile* programme in March 2013. In 2015 Devon Wildlife Trust became the lead partner in a five-year Lottery funded Horseshoe Bat project.

A four-foot cube is 64 cubic feet and weighs four tons

Horsepower at work in the quarries

Greater Horseshoe bats, some marked by Fiona, cluster in the caves

Nearby, in 2013, an experienced metal detectorist discovered fourth century Roman coins. Amazingly he went on to find 22,888 of these as well as three iron ingots. The coins, each at current rates worth about £2, came from 17 different mints in nine modern countries ranging from Syria and Egypt to France, Germany and London. Tom Cadbury, from the Royal Albert Memorial Museum in Exeter, won Heritage Lottery money and with the support of Clinton Devon Estates and varied donations from the public, managed to acquire the Hoard for the Museum. At the time of his talk to Seaton Visitor Centre Trust in 2017 no-one could produce a convincing account of why the coins were buried there at that time.

Across the estuary in Axmouth, once equally important to the Romans, John Mallock lived in Stepps House, one of the oldest buildings in the valley. In the 1670s he helped to finance the reclamation of Seaton Marshes by his brother-in-law John Willoughby. Stepps already had a long history but Stedcombe, another important Axmouth house, wasn't built until the 1680s. It is sited close to an earlier mansion which, when garrisoned for Parliament was burned to the ground in 1643. In 1988 Christopher Rae Scott bought Stedcombe, roofless after 25 years of total neglect. In three years he restored this unusually small example of the type of house developed by Sir Roger Pratt in the 1650s at Coleshill, Kingston Lacy and Clarendon in Piccadilly. Christopher maintained that "In its planning, detail and construction it closely resembles these much larger buildings but that the brick and stone belvedere which incorporates all the chimney flues is most unusual and probably, for its time, unique."

The earlier owners of Stedcombe were the Hallett family who had been among the first settlers in Barbados with John, from Lyme Regis, being listed as one of the 'Eminent Planters' in 1673. After the family bought the estate another John made plans, between 1803 and 1809, to stabilise the harbour entrance and attempted to make a port with £5000 of his own money. The work included a wall from upstream of the present bridges to the harbour entrance where a custom house was built; the existing Harbour House acted as a warehouse. With other walls directing ebb flow and suppressing wave surge, a prosperous little tidal port was established with ships of up to 150 tons engaged in coastal trade and weekly sailings to London. There was also a trade with the Mediterranean and the Canary Isles. In the 1840s Hallett's *Stedcombe* sailed to Australia.

Stepps House drawn for the cover of a Conservation Society Newsletter, 1997

Stedcombe House

Haven Cliff and the Custom House photographed in about 1904

> "Axmouth Harbour, which is highly favoured by nature, presents at this time, a very business like appearance. On Wednesday no less than four schooners entered here in splendid style and were soon moored in sheltered quarters."
> - *Western Times* 22nd August 1858

The writer believed that Axmouth might yet be destined to become a place of considerable importance, for its spacious harbour could be made one of the best on the English coast. However the difficulty remained 'for the shifting beach gives some little problem'. Four years later the *Taunton Advertiser and Western Courier*, 4th August, thought the inhabitants of Seaton were finally facing their own difficulties, "for at last they have aroused themselves from slumber and are opening their eyes to the necessity of doing something to render the place a residence for strangers. The public walk that has for sometime lain in a state of slovenly desolation is to be put into order and extended under the cliffs to the west."

A noble pile of buildings was being erected and a cricket club had been established 'promising to provide amusement for the old, recreation for the young and calculated to improve the moral as well as the physical condition of the inhabitants.' "There can be no doubt that these and other attractions will place Seaton amongst the first watering places on the Devonshire Coast."

Some years later, after the arrival of the railway and the building of Axmouth Bridge, a writer for *Pulman's*, 18th June 1879, reported that the growing population of Seaton, "that fashionable, favourite and delightful watering place faced a dilemma over their sewage", for if it was "allowed to wander of its own sweet will down the shingle and into the sea, the doctors inland would soon begin to send their patients to some other coastal resort. Having an eye for the salubrity of their town the worthy people thought it would be as well to make the mouth of the Axe do service for the discharge of the river water and the refuse of Seaton."

But Mr Hallett, Lord of the Manor of Axmouth, had other ideas and Pulman's correspondent, with tongue in cheek, observed 'that the Seaton authorities are surprised that such a place as Axmouth still exists. They live within a mile of it and have always been under the impression that it was as dead as the Romans and other ancient people who used it.'

Mr Hallett was far from dead, he knew the river, and pointed out that other than at high tide the water did little better than percolate through the shingle bar so that the lower part of the stream was nothing less than an enclosed pool. He contended that if the sewage 'is poured into this pool it will never get to the sea at all and the befouling of the stream would severely injure property.' *Pulman's* reckoned that if they weren't between two fires the people of Seaton were between two waters, unable to get either.

Axmouth Harbour around 1860

Whitecliff, 1880

In *The Book of The Axe* (fourth edition 1875) Pulman thought that Hallett should have had government aid but none materialised "and although for a time small vessels were able to enter and some trade was done, the sea, not being sufficiently resisted, went on with its work, the pier became shabby and the harbour a thing of the past." Things were not helped by the arrival of the railway with Seaton Junction, initially Colyton for Seaton, opening in 1860. Three years later an Act was passed sanctioning a branch line to Seaton and a bridge over the Axe. Before the Seaton and Beer railway company opened the line, along the existing Willoughby bank, there was an objection by Sir Walter Trevelyan, Lord of the Manor of Seaton and with other extensive estates, to widening the embankment on the west side as it would interfere with drainage he had carried out in the 1850s. Instead it was widened by 3 m to the east, using clay from the channel dug out from the estuary parallel with the bank. Today the tramline is on the bank and Redshank feed in the channel. In the *Proceedings of the Devonshire Association* (1985) Margaret Parkinson pointed out "that problems of financing the railway itself prevented early action regarding Axmouth Bridge but at the end of 1875 the directors of the railway company authorised raising £3000 of Axmouth Bridge stock. The bridge, reputedly the first in Britain to be built of concrete was opened as a toll bridge in April 1877." When Station Road was built it continued over Axmouth Bridge, the piers of which much reduced tidal flow thereby helping to change the estuary ecosystem. With the road in place development on its northerly marshy side, and on the shingle backslope followed.

Trevelyan Road had been built across this backslope to give visitors an easy route from the station to the beach but once on the beach the Trevelyans remained well in control as a poster stated "the Lord of the Manor reserves himself the right to prohibit the use of his beach in any particular and at his pleasure."

Pulman's view of a relatively treeless Hawkesdown Hill above Axmouth

Seaton Bay and the Railway, c.1905

A NEW CENTURY

> "The sea in front of me is playing a great symphony as the long waves break upon the pebbly beach of varying colours. The surface of this delightful sweep of water, forming one of the prettiest bays on Devon's coast, was broken by the gentlest ripples. I gazed down from Whitecliff and marvel at the fantastic pictures formed by the seaweed below." *Exeter and Plymouth Gazette*, 19th March 1902.

"Gone is the ferry, gone is the trade of Axmouth Harbour" continued the Gazette but the toll for crossing the river remained. A protester in the *Western Times* in 1905 deplored the toll as an anachronism that meant that Axmouth people "hurrying to the train must feel in their pockets for bridge money."

Tollgate on Axmouth Bridge 1904

By the end of 1906 a significant part of the large sum that Lady Alice Trevelyan demanded for the sale of the bridge had been raised but the Gazette reported that apathy ruled in Seaton with the people in the town refusing to make any offer and dead against anything being done. In Axmouth however, they were planning a celebratory meat tea, at a shilling an adult, six weeks before the freeing. By the actual date of the freeing, 30th September 1907, members of Seaton Urban District Council were among those on the temporary platform as the town band struck up "see the conquering hero comes". This hero had given £2200 to the cause and after 35 years the toll was freed. "Largely due to the munificent generosity of Mr S Sanders Stephens JP CC".

Once Mr Stephens, successor to the Halletts at Stedcombe Manor, had declared the bridge free, some sturdy supporters proceeded to burn the toll gates. Mr A W Oakley, Chairman of the District Council then spoke about "another blessing he would like to see, viz the river mouth freed. In years gone by big ships used to enter the River Axe, now there were none. He would like to see big steamers coming into the harbour (laughter and calls of hear hear!)" David Clarke's 1995 painting is a clear indication Mr Oakley's hopes were not to be realised. However in 2017-18 great improvements to access and fish storage were made with help from the Blue Marine foundation.

c. 1905 Seaton seafront and Haven Cliff

Low tide, Axmouth Harbour, 1995

Following his comments about Hallett's pier becoming shoddy Pulman wrote in 1875 "that a considerable portion of the inner pier, forming a portion of the old work was washed away in a gale on Sunday, January 31st 1869. Prior to the creation of the pier, about 1803, the river did not regularly flow into the sea but remained held back ... and overflowed a portion of the marsh which now lets at £7 or £8 an acre and then for five shillings only."

The increase in value was also due to improved drainage, for, in the 1850s Sir Walter Trevelyan had created a pattern of herringbone drains using 200,000 tiles.

With the arrival of the railway, restoration of the harbour was uneconomic, its entrance continued to narrow and not until the 1930s did a few boating pioneers begin to bring it back to life. In 1936 they formed the Seaton Sailing and Motorboat Club which was reconstituted after the war as the Axe Yacht Club. The Stedcombe estate sold the harbour to Axminster RDC in 1967 and seven years later it became the property of the EDDC. The Council, supported by volunteers, started regeneration and today the harbour company, formed in 1988, holds a lease from the council which sub leases to the club and the Fishermen's Association. In April 2013 the Axe Vale Canoe Club opened their refurbished club house in the grounds of the Yacht Club.

Back in 1934 the solicitors of Lady Alice Trevelyan had been approached by a company which had established a chalet type holiday camp at Hayling Island and wanted a similar setup in Seaton. Low-lying land close to the station was sold to the company and Warners opened the camp ready for Easter 1936. Two years later Lady Alice sold the remainder of the reclaimed marshes, and plots known as Great and Little Ragged Jack were bought by Seaton UDC. These two plots were later to form the core of Seaton Marshes Local Nature Reserve, now part of the Seaton Wetlands.

The 1938 Parliament Bill, which entitled all industrial workers to a week's paid holiday, helped post-war Seaton to develop the holiday camp which opened in 1959. Housebuilding created run-off into the marshes where floods, exacerbated by the failure to maintain tidal flaps following the closure of the railway in 1966, reached a peak two years later. These floods may well have been the stimulus for local councils to commission the Axmouth Feasibility Study to investigate the possibility of a large marina and tiers of holiday homes.

Axe Yacht Club: Mooring basin and lower pontoon

The Axe in flood

THE AXMOUTH STUDY 1971

Initially the London-based consulting engineers who produced the Axmouth study in November 1971 optimistically thought that access to the harbour from the sea could be through the shingle below the concrete bridge. The works would have been substantial as a breakwater sitting in deep water would have been essential and the cost would run into millions of pounds. Instead they turned their attention to the marshes thinking that "the situation of the marshes with their relatively small area lends itself to the formation of a lake whose periphery could be developed in such a way as to enhance the natural beauty of the valley. This would include, in a carefully landscaped setting, recreational facilities. The accommodation, holiday homes, further enhancing the natural beauty, would be built in ascending tiers, away from the water's edge. Landscaped islands would enhance the 70-80 acre lake on which you could have 150 small boats. As well as a small hotel or botel about two hundred small homes and flats could be built as closely bordering the lake as possible."

These houses would have been on the western edge, with a mooring basin, fishing lake, bowling green, bandstand, swimming pool, tennis court, car park and restaurants to the south. To the east nature walks were planned and other gestures towards the environment were to be a ban on motorboats and water-skiing and no "free for all" in houseboats. When a helicopter pad was mooted it was felt that "the disturbance it would cause would be enough to rule it out."

One result of the opposition to the plan, which was probably rejected because of cost, was the formation of the Axe Vale and District Conservation Society. Its Little Egret logo was not adopted until years later when this colonist became established on the estuary. Opposition to the loss of wetlands was vital for, on a national scale, the 1970s were to see the area affected by grant aided drainage schemes rise fourfold to some 100,000 hectares.

Plaque on the concrete bridge:

> Scheduled Ancient Monument
> Axmouth Old Bridge
> Opened 1877
> Closed to Traffic 1990
> This is the oldest standing concrete bridge in England

Different sorts of islands are now a feature of Black Hole Marsh in the Seaton Wetlands

The new bridge over the Axe was opened in 1990

CONSERVATION INITIATIVES

The local conservation society was formed following a meeting in the Feoffee's Hall in Colyton on 6 November 1973. None of the earliest newsletters are available but number 11, Autumn 1980, reported that South West Water planned to construct an earthwork across the marshes to prevent flooding in Seaton. The writer feared that if the marshes dried out any more there would be further attempts to develop the area. By the time of the next newsletter the Society had been backed by the Nature Conservancy Council in suggesting safeguards for the estuary. These had been written into the East Devon Heritage Coast Study and the marshes, up to Coly Bridge, named as an area of special ornithological importance.

The Borrow Pit, dug out to provide material for the flood defence wall, was let to the society which had persuaded South West Water to leave an island in the middle. Philip and Moraig Noakes, much involved in all the negotiations, would supervise planting around the pit. From a possible crisis came the start of the Seaton Wetlands which will continue to develop.

Bruckland Valley Lakes

Reaching the island in the Borrow Pit

Newsletter 15 reckoned that the story of the marshes "unfurls week by week like one of those television soap operas" with Seaton Town Council having modified their plans "for a cultivated area with park, trees, water and a lagoon for fishing and boating" whereas the views of the Society didn't change – open marshland should be left. By 1988, Philip, now chairman, feared that the character of the marshes was changing as more drains were put in at the expense of reedbeds. For his work as Consul General in Seattle he had been awarded the OBE and his Times obituary mentions the brevity, variety, wit and natural authority of his letters to the paper.

A bigger threat to tributary valleys came when South West Water planned to take water from the Axe, near Whitford, to fill a new reservoir either in the valley of the Stafford Brook or of the Bruckland stream. As ground surveys and test drilling progressed alarm and despondency grew.

Later the water authorities adopted different plans and later still, downstream at Lower Bruckland a series of landscaped lakes were dug out and became a haven for dragonflies and a lovely spot for birds and views.

The Small Red-eyed Damsel, first recorded in Britain in 1999

Common Darters mating

By 2009 these lakes had become one of the 60 key dragonfly sites in Devon with Small Red-eyed Damselflies breeding, Red-veined Darters sometimes breeding and Scarce Chasers and Red-eyed Damselflies probably doing so. None of the species were found on a grey August day in 2013 when Dave Smallshire introduced his course on "the identification and ecology of dragonflies" with the four adjectives on the side header. The day ended at the ponds where, by the fast, strong Bruckland stream, two species characteristic of that habitat were soon found. These were a male Beautiful Demoiselle, with dark iridescent wings, and a Golden-ringed Dragonfly which wisely hung vertically under sheltering ivy leaves.

By the very different, slow flowing and muddy river Axe, just north of the A3052, several male Banded Demoiselles fluttered over the water and rank riverside vegetation. A female with beautiful metallic green thorax and abdomen was caught, studied and released as were several White-legged Damselflies which differ from the other blue damsels in the expanded wide edges to their legs.

Earlier in the day, after a talk in the wetlands classroom, Dave, with no high hopes because of the weather, had taken participants out onto rough ground nearby. He described how, on such a day, both damsels and dragonflies would lurk inconspicuously in sheltered scrub or under tree leaves. Not only were three blue damsel species found, Common Blue, Blue-tailed and the splendid Azure Damselfly but attentive eyes located sheltering Common Darter. The Ruddy Darter is a special dragonfly of Seaton Marshes where 18 species of Odonata, the order to which dragons and damsels belong, were found between 1997 and 2006.

These marshes, like the Axe between Kilmington and its confluence with the Coly, are also key Devon dragonfly sites. Local naturalists can make very useful contributions by sending records, particularly of proven breeding, to Dave at davesmalls@btinternet.com. Proof of breeding is best provided by finding exuviae as described in the book *Field Guide to the Dragonflies and Damselflies of Great Britain and Ireland*. Finding larvae or pre-flight emergent individuals is also good evidence. The British Dragonfly Society welcomes casual records with a site grid reference.

Male Beautiful Demoiselle (females have dark brown wings)

The Scarce Chaser, a nationally important species occurs at all three key local sites

> "When one is told that NERC has taken over NC and so is responsible for both NNR and SSSI but not AONB or NP there is an automatic implication that if one doesn't follow one is, indeed ignorant." - Sir Dudley Stamp in *Nature Conservation in Britain* (1969).

Since the Second World War a plethora of habitat designations linked to a baffling array of acronyms have cropped up around the estuary. Many of these are the result of the Parliamentary or European legislation ranging from the National Parks Act of 1949 to the Marine and Coastal Access Act of 2009 and beyond. Local government has also played a significant role with East Devon District Council creating Local Nature Reserves or LNRs for the protection of wildlife and for public enjoyment.

Enterprise Neptune has helped the National Trust to acquire much of the country's threatened coast. In West Dorset Burton Bradstock, Golden Cap and Stonebarrow are spectacular Trust properties while in East Devon extensive clifftop sites around and west of Branscombe are part of the wonderful 630 mile South West Coast Path. An old amenity society, the Sid Vale Association, was founded in 1846, and newer ones have grown around the valleys of the Otter, Axe and Lym. The Axe Vale and District Conservation Society has close links with the Seaton Wetlands, the Undercliffs NNR, East Devon AONB and Seaton Jurassic.

John Dower in his 1945 report on National Parks was among the first to recognise publicly the fine landscapes of East Devon and included much of it as an amenity area on a lower rung than a National Park. The newly elected Labour government established its National Parks Committee which extended Dower's Blackdown Hills and Sidmouth Bay amenity area, by adding coastal strips west from Sidmouth and east from Seaton into the Undercliffs. At this stage Budleigh Salterton, Colyton, Seaton and Sidmouth were included in the amenity area but the last three were later excluded from the East Devon Area of Outstanding Natural Beauty. It was perhaps regrettable that the Axe estuary was also excluded.

Colin Pady, Prof. Malcolm Hart and Councillor Ann Liverton 'opening' Holyford Woods, England's 1000th LNR

Peak Cliff, west of Sidmouth

Sidbury, in the heart of the east Devon AONB

CONSERVATION INITIATIVES

A priority for the National Parks Commission (NPC) was clearly to establish National Parks, but in 1953 a list of possible AONBs was also considered. Although not at first thought of as front runners for this status, the North, South and East Devon coastlines were discussed in November 1954. An Area of Special Landscape Value covering the East Devon plateau, including the Blackdown Hills and Pebblebed Heaths, was proposed but not until June 1956 was the reality of a local AONB investigated.

The Snowdon Horseshoe from Moel Siabod, in the first Welsh National Park

L J Watson, landscape architect and artist, who gave advice on landscape designations, seemed happy to exclude the Blackdowns, as queries about the value of their agricultural scenery had been expressed. He also had doubts about the inclusion of coastal towns, particularly with the intrusive caravan park west of Seaton. The NPC believed in the overriding importance of the coast and excluded the Axe and Coly valleys.

By 1962 much of the Axe Valley was back in the protected area. The Ordnance Survey was requested to produce a new map and "the fine and diverse landscapes of East Devon and its spectacular coast" became the 14th AONB on 20 September 1963. The process of designation had taken seven years but no special management service was proposed until, in 1984, the coastal strip became the East Devon Heritage Coast. This was one of 34 coastlines in England selected for their scenery under the guidance of geomorphologist Prof J A Steers who, like L J Watson, played a significant role in getting the Undercliffs designated as a National Nature Reserve. The success of the Heritage Coast Project encouraged the county and district councils to establish an AONB-wide management service.

Beer Head on the Heritage Coast

In 2000 the Countryside and Rights of Way Act strengthened the administration of AONBs with local authorities having to prepare and publish management plans.

The Partnership Plan for 2019-2024 has three strategic aims and objectives. The first important but rather obvious aim is to conserve and enhance the natural beauty of the area. The second goes under the heading "people and prosperity", supporting sustainable economic development, social engagement and recreational activity. Finally the plan wants to ensure that the AONB is recognised and valued and is effectively managed in partnership with the 21 local stakeholders such as AVDCS, Natural England, Clinton Devon Estates and the Environment Agency.

River Axe meanders in the East Devon AONB

CONSERVATION INITIATIVES

In 1991 the Stafford Brook running through Holyford Woods, just outside the AONB, was rejected as the water supply for the new reservoir and the valley of the Bruckland stream became the preferred site. However, two years later, the National Rivers Authority refused the application for this site as well, as mentioned in newsletter 35, but it did allow a licence for water extraction from the Exe to top up the Wimbleball reservoir. This was expected to cater for the needs of East Devon for at least 15 years.

This newsletter also reported on the society's involvement in Heritage Coast events, in the Undercliffs, along the estuary and at Trinity Hill where nightjars were the star attraction and where Buzzard, Meadow Pipit, Stonechat and Reed Bunting bred.

The establishment of Local Nature Reserves, possible since the National Parks Act of 1949, had been very slow but in 1994 the first in East Devon was planned for the heathland of Trinity Hill and another was proposed for Seaton Marshes. These had now become the responsibility of the newly formed National Rivers Authority.

Management vindicated as heather returns

In June 1993 a feasibility study to examine issues such as habitat creation and improvement, access and archaeology in Seaton Marshes had been commissioned. This led to an appraisal of the past salt industry and to dragonfly and ditch surveys by ecologist Lesley Kerry who produced a management plan in 1997. As he reached 80 and completed a protracted period of rehabilitation following a hip replacement, Philip Noakes aimed to ease up. New to Devon I suddenly found myself Chairman of the Society and being questioned about the District Council's management of Trinity Hill and the limited level of activities for members.

The removal of bracken rhizomes at Trinity Hill caused some consternation

In response to the second question twenty three events were arranged for the summer of 1996 with Ian Waite leading the first walk to enjoy the bluebells in Holyford Woods on 24th April. For the next 20 years, before a stroke, he led walks for the society with the emphasis on birds. His role has been taken over by Rob Johnson whether on Dartmoor or at one of the Dorset or Devon estuaries. Also in 1996 a series of work parties, particularly in the Undercliffs and Local Nature Reserves, were added to the Society's programme.

Councillor Bill Waterworth opens the first simple hide at Seaton Marshes

CONSERVATION INITIATIVES

Drake Garganey

Lesley Kerry was involved again when Geoff Jones, Rural Affairs Officer for the District Council, and I, met her to discuss management in and around the Borrow Pit. The meeting was enhanced by fine view of a male Garganey. Later in the year the Conservation Society committee gave their support to the development of the Seaton Marshes reserve, even if formal approval of reserve status had not yet been granted by English Nature.

Geoff booked Seaton Town Hall for a meeting on 9th September to give the public details of the plans for the area and he hoped that, by the time of the meeting, there would be more certainty about future management. These plans would be based on Lesley's earlier work and the archaeological appraisal previously mentioned. It was not until October 2001 that the second management plan was drawn up by Ian Crowe. He was keen that the reserve should be managed in the context of the estuary as a whole and that the objectives should be measurable and able to be monitored. The first objective was "to create favourable over-wintering habitat for wetland birds". Favourable conditions would be seen to be achieved if the "weekly peak counts of Wigeon reached 50, if grass height between October and March was at, or below, 5 cm and if, over the same period, flooding in creeks and low-lying areas was permanent over a large part of the reserve."

Among 24 objectives were those of restoring grazing marsh habitats, monitoring Little Grebe habitat in the Borrow Pit and confirming the number of breeding dragonfly species as well as informing the public about wildlife. To achieve the first of these, ideal conditions for breeding Redshank and Skylark needed to be created but while both require an adequate food supply close to the breeding site Redshank need short open grassland in combination with damp conditions while Skylarks need it to be drier and with longer grass of 10 cm or more. This shows something of the difficulty of achieving action plan targets but over the years the marshes have done well even with times of neglect, and even when no Redshank or Skylark breed.

Ian Crowe's Ruby Red cattle play an important part in marsh management

Broad-bodied Chasers are bulky dragonflies favouring small ponds

Little Grebes breed regularly

Birds around the estuary have received attention since Pulman's *Book of the Axe* but those out in Lyme Bay were less well-known, so that a small initiative by AVDCS birdwatchers in September 2000 seemed appropriate. Armed with

Bird watchers in Lyme Bay

smelly, macerated mackerel they set out in Harry May's *Predator* and, when almost out of sight of land, were surrounded by diving Gannets with Shearwaters and Skuas all around the boat. Since then Tom Brereton, research director of the charity "Marine Life", is among those who have recorded the wealth of life in the Bay. Over 100 records of White-beaked Dolphins have accumulated since 2007 which is most unexpected as this is a cold water species. The most likely dolphin to be seen from land is the Bottlenose but at sea Risso's is possible as are Harbour Porpoises.

Little was known about populations of these species in 2000 and there was even less understanding of life permanently beneath the waves. Luckily Devon Wildlife Trust was already investigating the rich but vulnerable life in the Bay. Chris Davis, then the Trust's project officer, told a meeting in Seaton about the diverse life in the shallow water. Tompot Blennys, vicious Velvet Swimming Crabs, Snakelocks Anemones, partly fuelled by their symbiotic algae and Devonshire Cup-corals, with skeletons of calcium carbonate, could be found.

Deeper down, among the kelp, life was influenced by dwindling light and the nature of the currents. Chris told of thousands of Peacock Worms and Trumpet Anemones a hundred metres off the Undercliffs and of the Yellow Boring-sponge, one of 70 sponge species in the Bay. Dahlia Anemones

The Devonshire Cup-coral is our only common stony coral

carpeted the bottom gullies. Where it was totally dark, as on the reefs with which Chris was particularly concerned, there were seven of the nine species of UK corals, a high diversity of sea squirts and, where currents flowed, abundant Plumose Anemones. The rare Sunset Coral, with the diameter of a

50p coin, had been found a mile off Lyme Regis and the Pink Sea-fan was, in theory, specially protected.

Chris's job, working with fishermen, councillors and conservationists was to negotiate and establish areas voluntarily closed to fishing. Sadly such agreements were not to prove the long-term answer. Eventually the 2009 Marine and Coastal Access Act began to give the marine environment some of the protection well established on land. Marine Protected Areas established by this act only applied to the bottom dwelling fauna so the publicity provided by a television programme in November 2014, featuring 80 dolphins, much enjoyed on one of Harry May's trips, emphasised the need for the establishment of the Marine Conservation Zone in the centre of Lyme Bay.

The Velvet Swimming-crab, with bright red eyes

Dahlia Anemones are powerful predators

The reality of disaster and the positive reaction that can follow was described by farmer Bill Short when foot and mouth disease struck in Membury on 12 April 2001. "One night, a glow in the sky soon after a windless day of low cloud and awful scent of burning flesh, coal and railway sleepers". But Bill always sees a way forward and continued "Good always comes after bad. After five years of crisis with BSE, declining export markets, low prices barely covering production and then the foot and mouth tragedy it is vital that there is incentive and hope. It is important for us all to think about the future, for our agriculture, countryside and all associated wildlife".

Bill Short and an AVDCS team with nest boxes for his woods

Another farmer, Colin Pady, not only thought about the countryside but acted when Holyford Woods were put up for sale by South West Water. Colin, fearing an unsympathetic purchaser, revived the Holyford Woodland Trust which had earlier opposed the reservoir scheme, and sought pledges to help to buy the woods. When £30,000 was quickly promised the District Council made up the sale price.

Another article in newsletter 52, about grassland management in the Undercliffs "gave an indication of the growing links between the Society and English Nature." These links have continued to develop as management projects have evolved and English Nature has become Natural England.

Links with the Council's Countryside Service were described by Fraser Rush, delighted at the response to his suggestion of a voluntary wardening scheme at Seaton Marshes. Fraser had taken the plunge in leaving Devon Wildlife Trust to look after five Local Nature Reserves about which he knew very little. Within no time he had created freshwater scrapes, a larger deeper lagoon, 11 earth banks with associated pipework and "a very muddy local nature reserve". Much of the mud was around the Borrow Pit where material dug out from the lagoon was used as infill to make the banks less steep, and therefore better for wildlife, once Fraser had used his old, almost forgotten fishing rod to help calculations!

The Council was initially less popular in the context of Seaton Hole where cliff falls in autumn 2000 had blocked access to the beach.

How much material dug from the new lagoon will fit in the Borrow Pit?

CONSERVATION INITIATIVES

At the AGM of the Seaton Development Trust on 9th March 2001 Jean Kreiseler expected to hear the Council would be making alternative access to the beach in the spring. Instead she heard that the policy committee had decided to do nothing. "This was unacceptable. To allow this to happen would mean that access would be lost forever. Liz Bruce suggested a petition, we formed the 'Save Seaton Hole Group' and District Councillor Margaret Rogers gave us her full support. On 30th of March we rather nervously began collecting signatures in Seaton."

By 18th April the final count revealed that 5214 people had supported the petition. A week later the group gathered at The Knowle for a full council meeting. At the same time letters had been written to councillors pointing out that vast sums of money were not necessary as all that was needed was a set of steps to the side of, and some distance, from the fall.

In the meantime, despite fences and 'footpath closed' notices people continued to scramble up and down over the fall. At the beginning of June, local residents Connie and Gordon Worthington became increasingly worried that there would be an accident and so Gordon, at the age of 81, set to work, unbeknown to the Council and, with a couple of mates dug out and set steps down the cliff. The Council described this activity as "trespass, damage to public property and threatening public safety" but they were forced to make a decision and on 17th June an emergency meeting allocated £7500 to contractors to remove the unofficial steps and replace them with official ones.

Jean's article finished "if you have never been to Seaton Hole please go down to the beach sometime. Watch the sea, listen to the rhythmic sound of the waves. Bird watch. Beachcomb. Roll up your trousers and go rock pooling. If you have grandchildren take them: if not, so what".

Seaton Beach Huts

Fulmars breed at Seaton Hole

The small but spectacular Tompot Blenny likes the rockpools

BTO BIRD SURVEYS

"BTO work is birding at the sharp end, where it really matters!" - John Woodland, British Trust for Ornithology, in Newsletter 51.

In 1994, at John's suggestion I began five years of Common Bird Census or CBC work in the vicinity of Goat Island. At that time this national project gave the best indication of bird populations and their changes in woodlands and on farms. Each year's counts involved 10 breeding season visits, during each of which every bird seen or heard was recorded on a large-scale map and, if all went well, for most species, the records appeared in clumps which represented breeding territories.

Relative abundance of common bird species in the Undercliffs NNR

	CBC mean %	BTO Atlas %
Wren	12.5	12.4
Chiffchaff	11.2	8.6
Blackcap	11.1	9.1
Robin	9.6	8.2
Blackbird	8.3	9.0
Wood Pigeon	5.5	6.3

Blue Tits accounted for 5.7% of records

Surveys for the 2007-2011 Atlas were simpler with counts of species in 2km by 2 km tetrads. In all 91,800 tetrads were surveyed by 40,000 volunteers who made 16 million observations. Soon after starting the 1994 Undercliffs counts I became involved in keeping monthly records of birds around the estuary as one of several thousand volunteers contributing to the Wetland Bird Survey.

The WeBS covered most British estuaries and many inland waters. Apart from covering the east side of the estuary and the two local nature reserves, access to the extremely wet and sometimes hazardous Colyford Marsh was important. Up to 100 Snipe and 200 Teal may lie low there while Wigeon and Green Sandpiper, invisible from the Colyford Common hide, are often to be found along the river.

While WeBS is mainly concerned with the estuary regulars, many birdwatchers like their rarities and between 2001 and 2003 Great-white Egret, Spoonbill, Marsh Harrier, Goshawk, Pectoral Sandpiper, Wryneck, Dartford Warbler and Bearded Tit were among 167 species identified. David Walters' newsletters kept people informed and in 2004 he produced his own report

The wonderful WeBS logo

In an area of woodland 14 Bullfinches (X) and 22 Marsh Tits (●) were recorded in ten visits. Likely territories are indicated

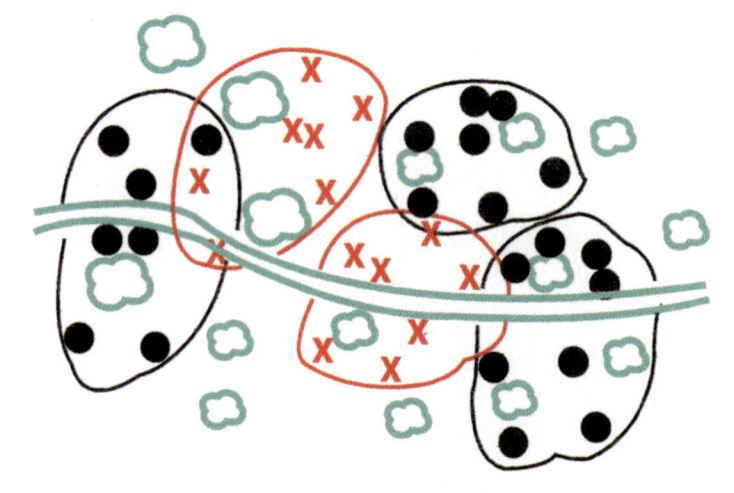

In this report David compared recent records from the local nature reserves with those reported in *Devon Birds* in 1966. Grey Partridge and Cirl Bunting had disappeared, Bewick's Swans and Greylag Geese had become irregular and Skylarks were much reduced. By contrast Canada Geese, Little Egrets, Cetti's Warblers and Mediterranean Gulls had appeared and Peregrines had returned after the banning of organochlorine pesticides. Goldcrests, Blackcaps and Pied Wagtails increased.

The 2005 report had double the number of pages, included line drawings by Mike Langman, as well as counts of birds recorded by patient sea watchers.

Following David's example other birders thought "that the time was ripe to publish a high-quality local report". An editorial committee, working with David and Fraser, aimed to use records, not only from the estuary and the sea but also from those finding interesting migrants at Beer Head. 2007 was the best year yet for rare species and the report included accounts of the discovery and identification features of Audouin's and Bonaparte's Gulls. 2008 was quieter with 199 species rather than 212 but the ringing group, set up in 2006, increased their catch to over 1000 if recaptures were included.

The real feature of the year was the District Council's acquisition of 73 ha of Black Hole Marsh and 1.8 ha of Stafford Marsh. This was linked to work with the Environment Agency for carefully controlled flooding. One aspect of this was the installation of a self-regulating tide gate between the estuary and the marsh to control water levels and salinity in such a way as to optimise the invertebrate populations so important to many birds.

Night Heron

In 2006 a Night Heron, vagrant from Europe, featured on the cover of the first full local bird report.

Mediterranean Gull

Mediterranean Gulls are scarce but regular passage and winter visitors. 18 species of gull have been recorded around the Axe.

38 THE ESTUARY AND ITS WILDLIFE

In the estuary itself, where there are few green plants, detritus brought down by the river, and the bacteria which feed off it, support the invertebrate life which provides the birds with their energy. These invertebrates include annelids such as ragworms (Nereis spp.) which feed on seaweed and carrion, and lugworms (Arenicola marina) which filter organic material from mud. Tiny crustaceans like Corophium and molluscs such as Hydrobia may be abundant even if larger species, at lower density, may provide an equal mass of food. These larger species including snail-like gastropods and bivalves like the Lamellibranch, Scrobicularia.

Grey Heron and prey

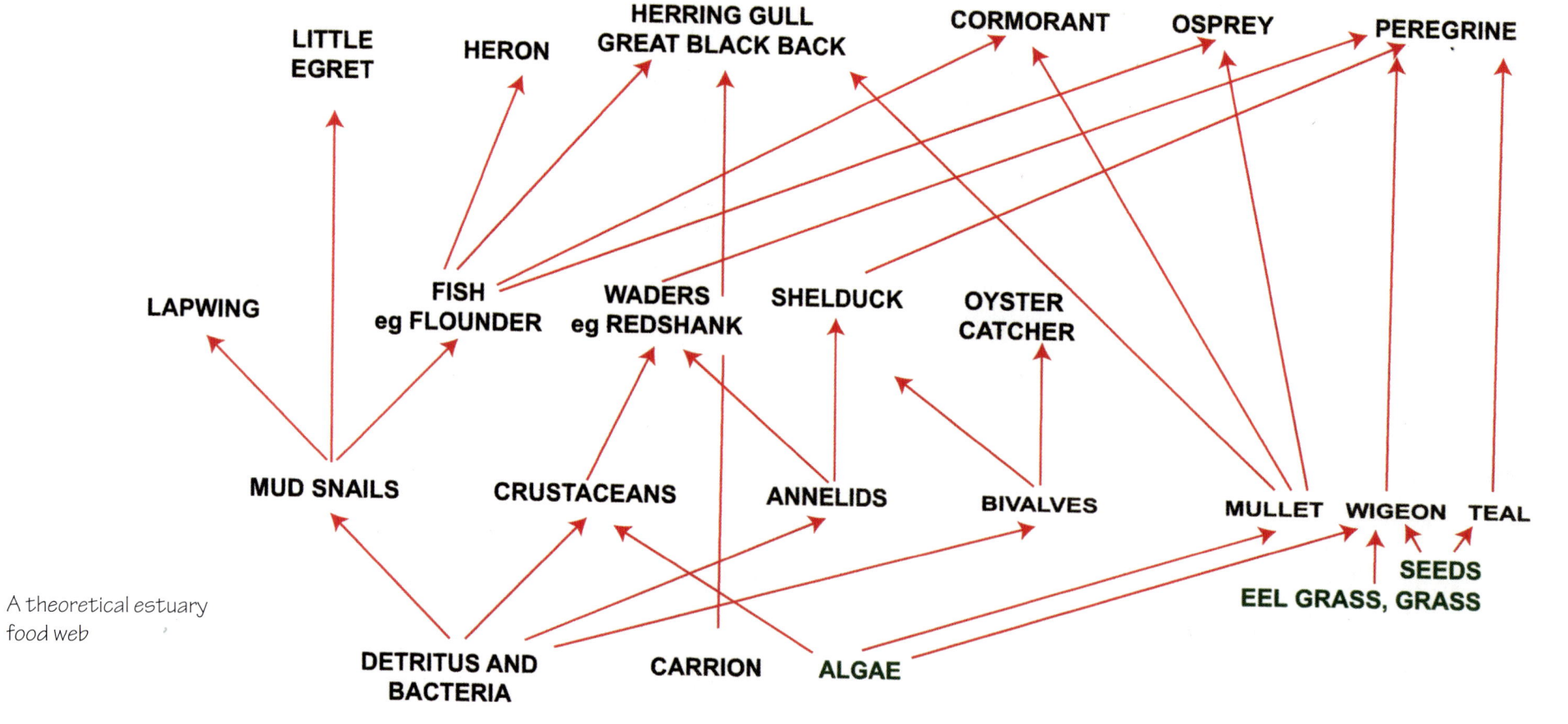

A theoretical estuary food web

THE ESTUARY AND ITS WILDLIFE

Ringed Plover feed on surface snails

Both bill size and structure have major influences on which prey species can be eaten. Ringed Plovers and Lapwings, with short bills, tend to feed by surface pecking, with the Lapwings doing much of their feeding at night if moonlight is sufficient. Dunlin can probe in the top 4 cm of mud reaching a wider range of prey while Redshank and particularly Curlew and the two Godwit species can reach greater depths. Watching Redshank from the Seaton Marshes hide one can often see them catching Ragworms high on the mud before taking them to the water for a wash before swallowing them.

Length of leg is equally important enabling a Black-tailed Godwit to feed in deeper water than a Bar-tailed, particularly as it has a longer bill. Both species may immerse their bills completely when feeding.

Many of the species mentioned are migrants either visiting in winter, like most of the Lapwings or passing through on passage like many of the scarcer waders such as Wood and Curlew Sandpipers, Ruff and Little Stint. Greenshank, with their lovely calls, are among my favourites. Passage passerines including Wheatear, Whinchat and Yellow Wagtail with the first two often spotted on fence posts and the Wagtail often looking for insects among, or on the feeding cattle.

Dunlin probe more deeply than plovers

The different bills and feeding techniques mean that a range of invertebrates are eaten.

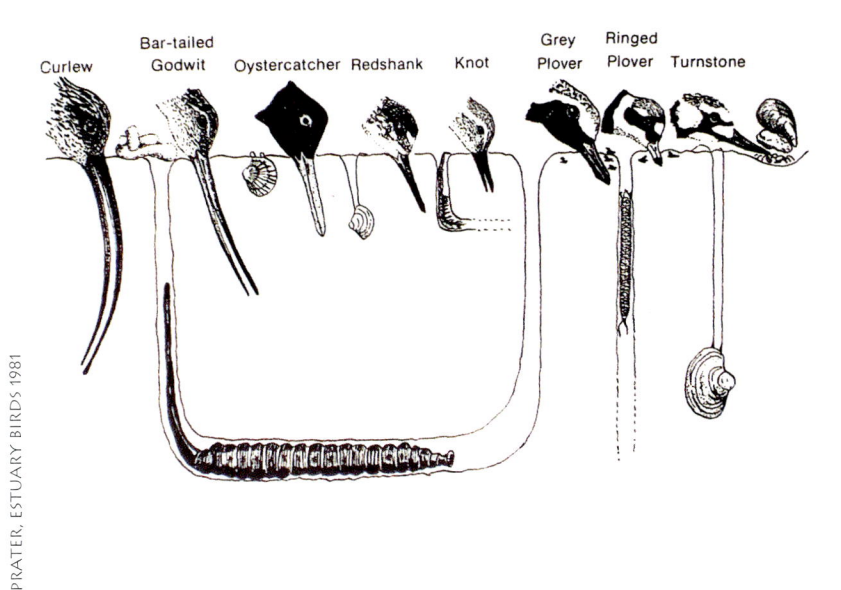

PRATER, ESTUARY BIRDS 1981

Passage Wheatears are often on fences and walkways approaching hides

A good way to see the estuary and its birds is to use the tram. Claude Lane, the enthusiastic founder of the Tramway, had driven trams in Llandudno in 1938. There had also been seasons in Hastings and Rhyl where he had been joined by a young Alan Gardner, later to succeed Claude as managing director in Seaton. The first miniature tram was built in Barnet where it was driven along a portable length of track at fetes and garden parties immediately after the war.

Wanting a long term base Claude settled in Eastbourne but plans for a new road forced him to think again and move elsewhere. The day after looking at potential track near Bridport, he drove down the east side of the estuary and immediately decided that the scenery and wildlife made the old railway embankment the perfect site.

Despite difficulties in buying the line he was running trams to Bobsworth Bridge, over the Stafford Brook, by May 1970. The line was extended to Colyford a year later and to Colyton in 1980. Private birdwatching trips began in 1984 and early in the new century similar trips for the paying public were introduced.

A very special trip for local councillors and representatives of Natural England and the Environment Agency passed the newly created Black Hole Marsh Lagoon on 2nd February 2009. Fraser Rush explained the background to this event in the annual Bird Report. "As plans for a large lagoon were being developed the Environment Agency launched a national project to create a new type of Self-Regulating Tide Gate (SRT) to allow carefully controlled tidal flooding of a wide range of sites all over Britain. Research and development of this project was largely based on Black Hole Marsh which is the prototype site for this first SRT."

Work on the new lagoon began in October 2008. 17 islands were created, some grassy, some muddy and some surfaced with a layer of shingle. A large new control sluice and embankment allow the independent management of its freshwater flooding so that dilutions of the saline lagoon can be avoided. The SRT was fitted in January 2009 and the lagoon flooded to its design depth of 300 mm (12 inches) with deeper sections up to 900 mm. Since then the tide gate has done everything that was in its design brief.

Tram passing Seaton Marshes Hide

Approaching the tram-shed

Tram beside the estuary

The Island Hide seen from the Tower Hide

The 'unmistakeable' Solitary Sandpiper with long and tapering silhouette

The agency's "fancy bit of kit" was admired as the tram headed up the estuary. Mike Williams explained that the tide gate allowed limited tidal flooding of the lagoon on spring tides so that there would be some tidal effect on an average of five days in every 14. The sites of future hides were pointed out. One of these, the Island Hide, needed to be opened slightly early when in 2010 bird watchers converged on the marsh to see the first Solitary Sandpiper in mainland Britain for 60 years.

Equally rare was a 13-Spot Ladybird found during a bioblitz in 2011. After being discovered as a larva on 31st July it was reared to adulthood and identified as the first proven breeding record in England for 60 years. With grazed saltmarsh, tidal lagoons, old hedgerows, developing reedbeds and the very clean Stafford Brook providing a mosaic of habitats it was not surprising that 750 species were found on the day. Two invertebrate specialists are shown on p. 82.

Both the Tower Hide, with fine views of the river and across the estuary and the field classroom, now known as the Reed Base, were also opened that year with the Seaton Recorder, 2nd December 2011, describing the classroom as "sitting on stilts over the reed bed and accessed via an island boardwalk designed to create a magical wow factor entrance through the reed bed". Fraser Rush added that "the wooden building sits low in the floodplain and it has been designed to cope with flood events ... Rather than attempting to keep the water out, the building has been designed to allow water to flood in, and out again, with special valves at floor level to ensure that this can happen".

Floods in July 2012 soon put the classroom's valves to the test and made breeding success for ground nesting birds impossible.

The Reed Base, classroom with the 'Axe Factor'

42 THE ESTUARY AND ITS WILDLIFE

DEVELOPMENT AT BLACK HOLE MARSH

Some of Mike Hughes' illustrations of local wildlife in the Discovery Hut

JAMES HARRIS

"Mike Runs Rings Around the Estuary's Bird Populations"

This was the headline for an article in the *Western Morning News* on 25 July 2009. Photographer Richard Austin had been taking journalist Martin Heap to interview a series of animal experts which included bird ringer Mike Tyler. Talking to him made Martin realise "that ringing is a much more elaborate and responsible job then you would perhaps first think. For a start you have to be licensed – and that means undergoing long periods of training with the British Trust for Ornithology". The BTO has a network of more than 2500 licensed volunteers who ring almost a million birds every year.

Mike, chairman of the ringing group, which he had helped to establish in 2006, told Martin that when ringing, you identify birds as individuals and can trace their movements and their length of life. He went on to say that 20% of birds were ringed as nestlings whilst for the rest there were a number of trapping techniques. The majority are caught in fine mist nets loosely extended between two poles. Traps range from small spring ones, to large Abberton traps which catch ducks. Large nets propelled by cannons are sometimes used around the Axe.

Mike Tyler releases a House Martin from a mist net

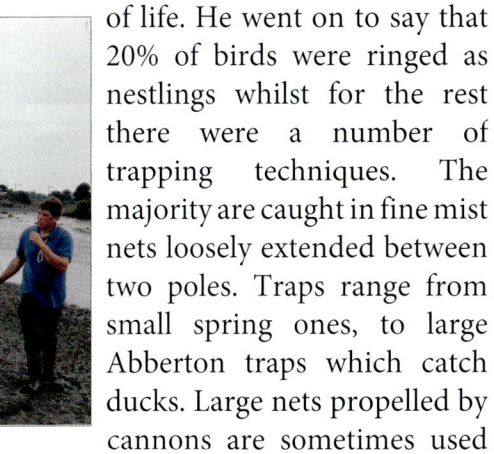

Neil Croton with mist net by the Axe

Water Pipits are easier to identify in the hand than in the field

In 2004 Mike and two of his trainees did some early morning ringing on Colyford Common and in the Tramway reedbeds. By the end of 2007, the first full year of the ringing group, there were only nine members but then numbers increased rapidly and more birds were ringed with at least forty species every year. Among these many Shelduck and Black-tailed Godwit were frequently retrapped. No colour ringed Shelduck were seen away from the marshes until six turned up in Bridgwater Bay where many go to moult.

Reed Warblers and Greenfinches were often the commonest catch but in 2006 cannon nets had caught 138 Wigeon, and four years later Teal were the top species with 133. One Wigeon had been ringed 4547 km away in Russia and since that recovery six more ringed Wigeon have been shot or found dead in Russia with one having travelled 4859 km. One Shoveler flew 2144 km before being shot, again in Russia and a Teal flew at least 3148 km before meeting the same end.

A Black-headed Gull which had been ringed in Poland was seen around the Axe a month later while a Common Gull from Norway turned up on the estuary 2418 km away after almost seven years. Mediterranean Gulls ringed in Denmark and the Czech Republic have had their rings read by observers on the Axe as well as being seen in Weymouth and Exmouth, Wales and France. Another well travelled bird on its way to Africa was an Osprey ringed as a pullus in Norway. 73 days after that it was over the estuary 1715 km away from its nest site.

Well over 100 Teal occur in winter

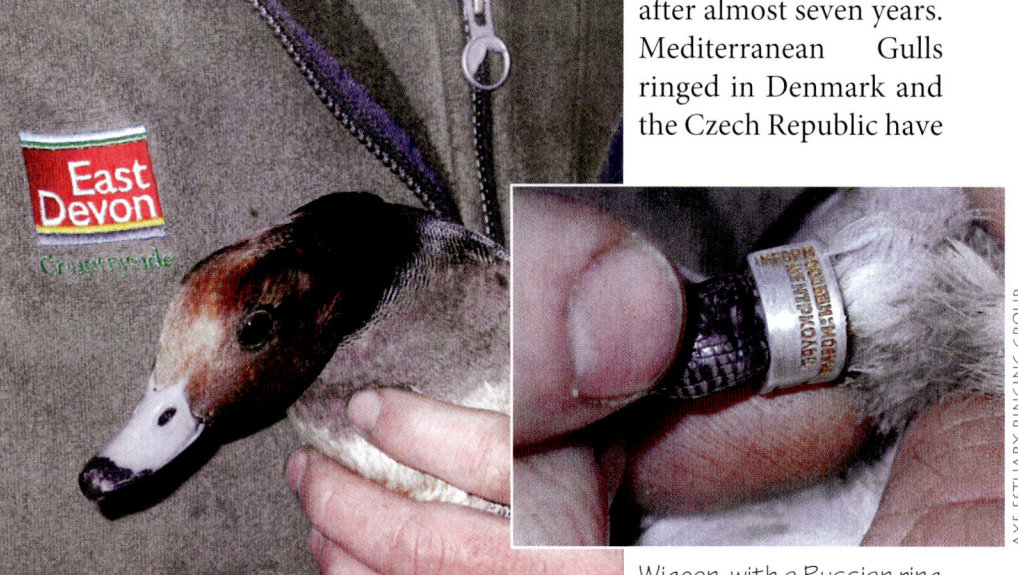

Osprey over Seaton

Wigeon, with a Russian ring

THE ESTUARY AND ITS WILDLIFE

Colour-ringed Black-tailed Godwits observed on the Axe have not only been seen at sites all over southern England but also in France, Orkney, the Netherlands and at their breeding sites in Iceland.

Wintering Godwits

Among smaller species a Wren moved 91 km in 102 days from Gwent to Colyford's crop field. A Sedge Warbler moved in the other direction going the same 91 km to Gwent where it was recaptured after 10 days. A final passerine example involved a young female Blackbird which was found dying in Antwerp 557 km from Colyford 48 days after being ringed.

Ringing also helps to age birds and six individuals of local interest have lived for at least ten years. An Oystercatcher, ringed on Bardsey, was recorded at Colyford 12 years and 121 days later. A Razorbill from Fair Isle and a Guillemot from Skomer both lived for over 11 years while a Chaffinch, also from Antwerp, lived eight years and 84 days before recovery in Seaton.

When tracing the movements of the individual bird, colour ringing can be particularly rewarding. The 2009 report told of 'a female Pale-bellied Brent Goose, ringed as an adult in south-west Iceland in May 2005 which was regularly seen during the following winters at Strangford Lough, Ireland, and in most summers near her ringing site. The last time she was noted in Ireland was on 11th August 2008 when in a large flock of Dark-bellied Brents, later with other Dark-bellied birds in Hampshire in January and February 2009 before visiting the Axe from 5-15th March.' Later she was seen again back in Ireland.

Axe Estuary Ringing Group members with Matt Baker and Julia Bradbury ready for Countryfile on 2nd March 2013

Despite periodic local breeding, few Redshank are ringed

Apart from the long-lived Bardsey bird, most Oystercatchers have been local

THE ESTUARY AND ITS WILDLIFE

Thrift, like Sea Aster and Scurvy Grass, is widespread on the reserve

Much of this section has told of birds around the estuary but the saltmarsh of Colyford Common is home to a range of other wildlife. As Fraser Rush described in newsletter 61 in 2006. "With most of the nature reserve lying at or near the top of the tidal gradient Colyford Common contains habitats which are regionally very scarce. These in turn support a number of plants and animals which are scarce or rare.

Key to the importance of the LNR and adjacent areas are their tidal characteristics. At the upper end of the estuary there are few man-made features such as seawalls or embankments. But at Colyford Common each tide finds its natural height without restriction. With so many estuary marshes having been reclaimed the area around the local reserve is almost unique in having been preserved with a natural tidal gradient.

These rare tidal characteristics give rise to saltmarsh habitats which are also rare. In parts of the nature reserve it is possible to see the gradual transition between freshwater marsh and saltmarsh.

Many plants found at Colyford are uncommon or rare in Devon. These include Beaked Tassleweed, Strawberry Clover, Long-bracted Sedge and Brookweed. With such uncommon plant species and communities the Common supports a wealth of animal life much of which is also uncommon or rare.

The Ground Lackey-moth thrives here. This is the only known location for this salt march species outside south-east England. Another scarce saltmarsh resident is the Short-winged Conehead. This bush cricket can be seen in the extensive areas of Sea Club-rush. Not surprisingly the area is important for a range of estuary birds especially waders and wildfowl. Large flocks of Wigeon, often up to 750, are present in winter with small numbers of Teal and Shelduck. Wintering Water Pipits are a local specialty while the area is increasingly important for Otters."

Botanists Mike Lock and Roger Smith, the author of *A New Atlas of Devon Flora*, 2016, have added to the wetlands records reporting the nationally scarce Bulbous Foxtail, the rare Horned Pondweed and Hard Grass, another Devon rarity.

Some Otters have been remarkably tolerant of people

Short-winged Conehead

PLANT ZONATION

> "Saltmarsh and mudflats are among the more productive and structurally simple of all ecosystems, subject to the immensely powerful control of the daily tides". – Brian Moss in *The Broads,* New Naturalist 89 (2001)

On the other side of the estuary, away from the managed wetlands, a high tide may almost reach the road but as it retreats it exposes a narrow band of halophytic, salt tolerant plants. These form a halosere, where a sere is made up of the series of communities exposed to different conditions. Mike Lock describes the effect of the tide in his notes for an estuary stroll. "The rise and fall of the tide means that there is a gradual transition from the high tide line to the low tide mark. At the high tide mark plants are only occasionally inundated by salt water. At the low tide mark plants must not only endure long periods of submergence in salt water but also freshwater when the river is high. The range of conditions means that the plants are arranged in overlapping zones." Lowest down the shore is the brown seaweed zone where species of wrack, Fucus, occur where there are stones for attachment. Above is a green seaweed zone with species of Ulva and Enteromorpha (Sea Lettuce) on the mud or gravel surface.

Pioneer higher plants like Glasswort (G), Annual Sea-blite (AS) and sometimes Common Cord-grass are next. Moving up to the saltmarsh zone, which is flooded briefly at high water of spring tides, the community is made up of Purslane (P), Sea Aster (SA), Sea Plantain (SP), Sea Arrow-grass, Greater Sea-spurry, Thrift (T) and saltmarsh forms of the Red Fescue (RF).

The top of the strandline zone is flooded only on high spring tides particularly when there is a strong south-westerly wind and/or a lot of water coming down the river. Sea Couch-grass is common here, often with Spear-leaved Orache, Sea Beet, Perennial Sow-thistle, Sea Rush, Sea Mayweed, Sea Radish and Curled Dock.

Luckily the floods in 2012 which tested the wetlands classroom's special drainage valves didn't damage the new bird observation platform overlooking areas of mud and saltmarsh. The platform, at Coronation Corner, had been provided by initiatives in Axmouth village. The floods did provide a good photo opportunity showing Fraser in the water that flooded into the classroom.

Zonation recorded

Fraser contemplates the flood

Regardless of floods, and there were more early in 2014, the wetlands continued to develop with more than £500,000 of help from various sources. These were summarised by Doug Rudge at the Conservation Society's AGM in 2013. As Contracts Officer for the Countryside Service he was well placed to tell of the Council's belief that green tourism would help

Location of Sheep's Marsh

Wetlands Funding 2008 - 2013		
Section 106 (Tesco)	Acquisition of Black Hole Marsh	£118,000
East Devon District Council	Extensive and varied contributions	£116,236
Natural England	Island Hide and paths	£110,691
Making It Local	76% of Information Centre, 70% of car parks	£64,080
Devon County Council	Paths and board walks	£35,946
Environment Agency	62% of Black Hole Marsh lagoon	£25,000
AVDCS	33% of Tower Hide, 43% of Sand Martin cliff	£22,000
Devon Birdwatching Society	33% of Tower Hide, 13% of Information Centre	£15,000
East Devon AONB	11% of Information Centre	£6,035
Plus a number of smaller donations		

to lead to economic regeneration, and that the projects in the wetlands would provide a focus for community involvement.

Back in 2012 Doug had written about the plans for the 10 ha of Sheep's Marsh and produced a map showing two major lagoons adjacent to Seaton Marshes and some 4 ha of reedbeds in the south-west corner. In Newsletter 73 he admitted there was still a lot to be done "before we can start the earthworks, complete the transfer of land, finalise the preferred design, arrange for a professional flood risk assessment, obtain Environment Agency approval and obtain planning permission."

Earlier in 2014 major changes in the organisation of the countryside service marked the end of an era as Fraser Rush decided to concentrate on his own conservation and construction initiatives while Doug Rudge ended his four-year contract. However development continued and in 2015 a long-awaited section of the Stop Line Way, with its impressive bridge over the Stafford Brook, gave improved access to the marshes. Problems at Sheep's Marsh remained but so too did the ambitious plans and one day there will surely be access to part of the marshes from extended grounds of Seaton Jurassic.

The involvement of Prof J A Steers in the designation of both the East Devon Heritage Coast and the Undercliffs National Nature Reserve was mentioned on page 29. In *The Sea Coast* (1953) Volume 25 of the New Naturalist series he mentions that at Beer head "the unconformity is nearly all below water and since the cliffs above are wholly of Cretaceous rocks, falls of chalk fall directly onto the beach ... There is no part of the British coast on which exists such a great extent of wild vegetation."

In an earlier, 1950, New Naturalist title *The Wildflowers of Chalk and Limestone* J E Lousley described small but interesting chalk outliers in Devon where "the chalk forms fine sea cliffs and an undercliff with a magnificent flora. Most of the common downland herbs are here. In addition there is Blue Gromwell." He found that the maritime plants like Rock Sea-lavender, Rock Spurrey, Samphire and Portland Spurge added excitement. Of the eight thistle species around the cliff today he only mentioned the typical seaside Slender-headed Thistle, before commenting on the interest of Nottingham Catchfly and Gladdon. Purple Gromwell, as we now know it, is common along the path below the Hooken Undercliff. Lousley refers "to the rapid transition on the top of the cliff from chalk soil to the quite acidic clay which covers it inland. The narrow strip of downland turf, close-nibbled by rabbits, includes such plants as Rock Rose, Salad Burnet and Squinancywort." These remain as does the late flowering Autumn Ladies-tresses, a tiny orchid.

Branscombe potato 'plats' ca. 1920

In a recent, 2013, New Naturalist, Michael Proctor describes how, in the 1960s, the Hooken Undercliff was a patchwork of hawthorn scrub and grassland but that "the grassland has long since gone".

Barry Henwood (2012) found in *Reminiscences of an Elderly Entomologist* details of the butterflies that have also long since gone. On 6th June 1930 RP Demuth found 27 species in Branscombe Undercliff with abundant Wood Whites and Adonis Blues as well as Small Blue and three species of fritillary. The Small Blue has recently been found again and Wood Whites survive but they, like Green Hairstreak, Brown Argus, Dingy Skipper and Chalkhill Blue are far from abundant.

The national distribution of the Catchfly

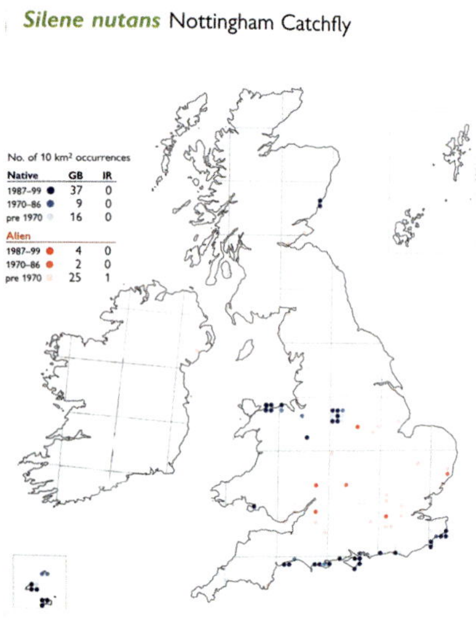

Autumn Ladies-tresses at Beer Head

Nottingham Catchfly

WEST TO BEER AND OUT TO THE SEA 51

The cliffs above the Underhooken are wholly of Cretaceous rocks

> "If we and the rest of the backboned animals were to disappear overnight the rest of the world would get on pretty well. But if invertebrates were to disappear the world's ecosystems would collapse". – Sir David Attenborough.

In addition to the butterflies the East Devon cliffs are home to many less familiar invertebrates. These are the business of the charity Buglife which is "conserving small things that run the world" by virtue of their roles in pollination and recycling, and their place near the base of food webs. Buglife points out that invertebrates favour rocks "that are poorly resistant to the natural processes that shape our coasts. Soft cliffs are formed of rocks such as clays, friable sands and glacial deposits contrasting with much more resistant hard rocks. The cliffs are subject to slumps and erosion by the sea and erosion above, by the rainstorms and groundwater seeping through the cliffs."

Geologist Richard Edmonds explains the history of mudslides on Black Ven

Soft cliffs at Black Ven

In the UK the soft cliffs are concentrated in England and Wales and the Sidmouth to West Bay Special Area of Conservation or SAC is amongst the most productive of these in terms of diversity and rarity of species.

All the active landslipping along the coast has created, and continues to shape, a mosaic of woodland, mixed scrub, grassland and pioneer communities. This makes the coast rich in burrowing solitary bees and wasps as well as flies which often depend on seepages for their aquatic larvae. Eroding parts of Haven Cliff, Pinhay Warren and Black Ven are ideal spots for thermophilic, warmth loving, invertebrates like the Ivy Bee and Cliff Tiger-beetle.

The citation for SAC status for Sidmouth to West Bay describes how "the site is an example of a highly unstable soft rock coastline subject to mudslides and landslips. The principal rock types are soft mudstones, clays and silty limestones with a small chalk outlier to the west. The eastern part of the Axmouth to Lyme Regis landslip has no chalk capping and is subject to mudslides in the waterlogged soft limestones and clays. Vegetation is very varied and includes pioneer communities on recent slips, calcareous scrub on detached chalk rocks and extensive self-sown woodlands dominated by ash."

Cliff Tiger-beetle

View over the picturesque and ancient village

> "Deep in a little winding combe among the cliffs which rear aloft their protecting heads in beautiful undulations and against the craggy faces of which the ocean beats incessantly, in vain, is situated the picturesque and ancient village of Beer." – George Pulman in *The Book of the Axe* fourth edition 1875.

Almost 140 years after that edition of *The Book of the Axe*, Beer beach was very busy on a sunlit May morning. Plenty of full English breakfasts were being eaten under umbrellas, the deckchairs were spread and beach hut doors were opening. The cliffs, studded with multicoloured flowers, Rock Sea-lavender, Sea Stock, Wild Cabbage, Tree Mallow and Wallflower were, in most places, too steep for a closed plant community.

The beach is shingle, but to the west are large, rounded, fossil rich boulders and, near the base of the cliff, distinctive blocks of Beer Head limestone. When the tide is out the Fine Foundation Heritage Centre organises rock pooling safaris as part of their broadly based education programme.

Beer Village Heritage (BVH) originated in 1997 when a wooden hut was erected on the beach and called Beer Marine Heritage Centre. The award of World Heritage status to the coast made BVH more ambitious, and they planned a new centre that was twice the size. It was up and running by April 2006. Volunteers contribute their time and skills and the centre, now known as the Fine Foundation Centre, has an aquarium looked after by the local fishermen, an account of the "Beer Boys" who rowed across the Atlantic and a piece of Beer Stone that has been into space. There are also expositions on Beer's smuggling, quarrying and lace-making traditions. For their part in promoting the Dorset and East Devon World Heritage Coast, through the activities of the Centre, Pat Farrell and Nora Jaggers were given special awards at the Jurassic Coast annual forum in 2010. Nora continues to be very active promoting the coast and, like Mike Green a real enthusiast for the coastal geology and East Devon's fossils, is a valued ambassador for the Jurassic Coast Trust.

Pat Farrell with rockpooling enthusiasts

The Fine Foundation Heritage Trust Centre

In February 2010 Beer Heritage Centre arranged the first meeting in Devon of what had previously been Dorset Coast Link. This aimed to share knowledge and to build skills relevant to conservation and education by linking the various centres along the Jurassic Coast.

Among the speakers was Jim Henton, chairman of East Devon fishermen and well-known locally as a fishmonger on Sea Hill. He reported on the fishing scene at Beer. Small single-handed boats that only go out for six miles or so are used; their size means that they can be pushed up and down the beach pebbles on greased wood runners.

Most of the fishermen were involved in sustainable crabbing with 100-150 pots. Skate and Sole were caught at different times of the year but "fishing was fishing" and versatility was needed when whelking, sea angling, diving and sightseeing were all seen as possible activities. Mackerel were now caught all year round and, at times, there were too many lobsters to keep the price high! There were not as many sprats as there had been at one time and Jim wondered whether this was due to an increase in Common Seals.

Fish available on Sea Hill

Seabass had become more frequent in the last 10 to 15 years. Beer fishermen had issues with bigger faster boats which move into their area when Axmouth or wherever is fished out.

With 60 square miles closed at that time to towed gear which damages the sea bottom, the reefs were becoming more productive. Scallops could then reach 80-140p each. Six or seven boats were operating out of Beer but only four were full-time and newcomers were unlikely as young fishermen want a harbour and not a beach haul. At one time Beer had the largest beach-based fleet of boats after Hastings.

The fishing at both Beer and Axmouth has recently benefited from the activities of the Blue Marine Foundation which has provided cold houses at the quays and cool boxes to take to sea so that the catch will be of optimum quality. Much of the catch will go for a good price at the prestige London market. The foundation exists to combat overfishing and the destruction of biodiversity partly by the creation of large marine reserves.

Fishing boats at Axmouth harbour supported by Blue Marine

Bass favour shallow, rocky areas

echinoderms and decapods while dive 59 revealed ledges and crevices full of crab species together with Spiny Squat-lobsters and Leopard-spotted Gobies. Boring and Goosebump Sponges were common.

Further out, between 15-20 m, the substrate is usually sandy and animal dominated, with Hermit Crabs and Netted Dog-whelks, but below 20 m large boulders and cobbles make up the best reefs which, in the absence of light, are also animal dominated. At that time Chris was concerned about habitat damage and its effects on certain species. The Pink Sea-fan, limited in England to the south-west, had substantial populations throughout the reefs. The brilliant yellow Sunset Cup-coral is one of our rarest marine species and there was a large and unusual sea squirt, Phallusia mamillata which he likened to a huge wax candle. There were lots of bryozoa (sea mats) and hydroids and the overall diversity made it one of the most interesting ecosystems.

Snakelocks anemones and Thongweed

In 2012 Devon Wildlife Trust celebrated 50 years of protecting wildlife and members received a calendar featuring the success of their reserves. The main image for July was a photograph by Paul Naylor of the seabed covered in Snakelocks Anemones with a Ballan Wrasse swimming between the pliable stems of the lower shore seaweed, Hymanthalia. It was this picture which led me to contact Paul, via the Trust, and soon he gave me access to the pictures which illustrate most of the sea life mentioned in this book.

His book *Great British Marine Animals* begins with descriptions of eight habitats, four of which occur close inshore in Lyme Bay. These are rocky reefs, both in shallow and deep water, rocky shores and sandy seabeds. The rocky shores off Culverhole Point had been investigated in 1994 when consultants surveyed 17 sites between Lulworth Cove and Axmouth as part of the Lyme Bay environmental study. On this exposed site they found 19 plant and 23 animal species among boulders on the mid-shore and 23 plant and 21 animal species lower down amongst the boulders and broken bed rock.

In the same vicinity, but just offshore, Chris Davis (page 32) had investigated two sites as part of his seabed mapping survey involving 88 dives. At 11 m depth both sites had sufficient light for brown and red algae but vertical bedrock faces were animal dominated. Dive 58 found crevice-dwelling

Pink Sea-fans branch at right angles to the prevailing current

Paul Gompertz, for many years director of Devon Wildlife Trust has written that "the first time I saw a picture of the reefs I thought I was looking at the marine life of some exotic and distant location. Within a short distance of our coast treasures abound. Sea fans, a delicate filigree of pink, and shaped like miniature trees, and grotesquely named Dead-men's Fingers as well as Cup Corals in delicate shades of gold together with Ross Coral shaped and coloured like a latticed brain."

Paul described how the reefs are invaluable as a nursing ground, water purification plant and feeding station. Although, as he said, many of the processes of the ocean are a mystery, there is growing realisation that our planet's future depends on the wildlife heartlands, the precious bits of largely unspoiled marine or terrestrial habitat where much of the real work of powering the Earth takes place.

Speaking at the Trust's AGM in 2010 Richard White, their Marine Advocacy Officer, told how, until the Marine and Coastal Areas Act of 2009 a Minister might establish an occasional marine protected area or MPA but since the Act he or she has a duty to designate a network of such areas. Some of these, Marine Conservation Zones or MCZ's, will be protected for social and economic reasons as well as habitat quality. Richard told the AGM that their location would depend on the issues of diverse stakeholders such as the aggregates industry, sea anglers, wind power developers and marine ecologists. In 2011, following unprecedented cooperation between the stakeholders, the government unveiled plans for 127 of these conservation zones. Their designation would prevent the most damaging forms of fishing, protect vital habitats and help the fishing fleet adapt to a more sustainable future. Late in 2012 the then fisheries Minister Richard Benyon approved a mere 31 sites including four in the south-west, Torbay with its sea grass beds, the Skerries Bank off Kingsbridge and two areas of the Tamar. In 2016 two more North Coast sites, Hartland Point to Tintagel and 40 miles between Bideford and Foreland Point were among 19 new MCZs. On 20th July 2018 consultation on 41 zones including five estuaries and three areas of the North Coast was completed and these were later designated.

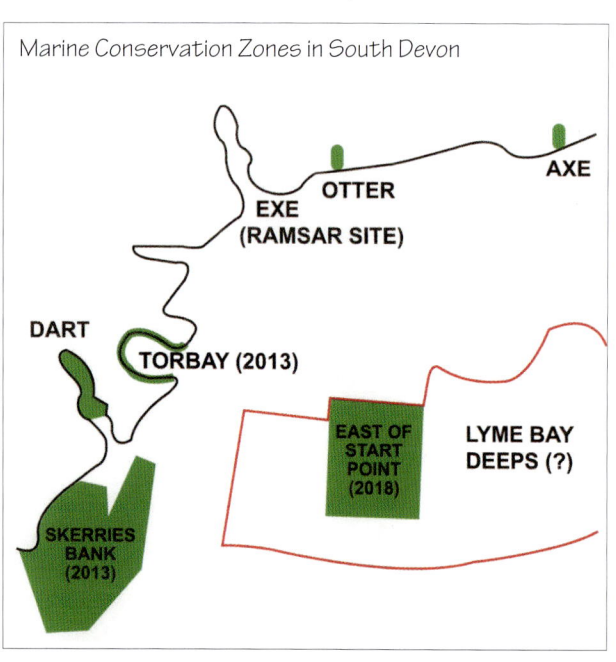

Ross Coral, or the Potato-crisp bryozoan, is a stationary colony of tiny animals

PAUL NAYLOR

Marine Conservation Zones in South Devon

Cliffs on the eastern side of Lundy bound the UK's first MCZ (2010)

ROGER KEY

A Great Scallop

Corals, anemones and sponges also increased providing critical habitat for fish and shellfish so that landings of Edible Crab in 2014 have increased two and a half times compared to 2008.

These figures were quoted in Marshwood Vale magazine, August 2018, where Dr Owen Day wrote that although the reserve was primarily aimed at the conservation of Ross Corals and Sea Fans "the ban on trawling and scallop dredging not only allowed these and other delicate organisms to recover but also led to a rapid increase in the numbers of lobsters, crabs, cuttlefish, sole and plaice that rely on a stable undisturbed seabed for food and shelter."

A major player in this success story is the Blue Marine Foundation which, in 2012, set up a local group of scientists, fisheries managers and fishermen. Initial meetings were challenging but conflicts were overcome.

Like the wildlife trust the Marine Institute of Plymouth University has been much involved in researching Lyme Bay. In a 2013 article Dr Emma Sheehan tells how the Institute, researching population changes following protection, used a towed flying video array to survey 200 m x 0.5 m transects in a non-destructive way. The report indicates that this was far from simple! Back in 2001 the severely damaged reefs at Beer Home Ground and the smaller Eastern Heads Reef, both within 5 km of Axmouth Bridge, had nominally been closed to dredging for Scallops. The marine life of these areas, 22 km², described as "closed controls" was compared to that in the 206 km² of Marine Protected Area established in 2008 and considered as "new closure". Sheehan's report found that the populations of Pink Sea-fans were still fluctuating in "new closure" areas but there were significant increases in the coral, Dead-men's Fingers and in King Scallops, as well as an increase in the primitive chordate Phallusia mamillata, a Sea Squirt, and some increase in the reef building bryozoan, Ross Coral.

Now the marine biologists from Plymouth have experienced 10 years of monitoring and found an eightfold increase in Sea Fans while King Scallops were seven times as abundant inside the Lyme Bay conservation reserve.

Lobster, with bright red antennae

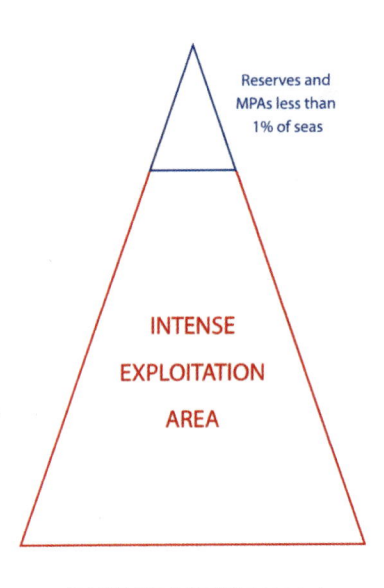

The success of Blue Marine in resolving major reservations of the fishermen operating from Beer, Axmouth, Lyme and West Bay led to a voluntary code of conduct. An important aspect of this is the fitting of tracking devices to monitor where fishing occurs, so that the catch can be labelled as "fully traceable". Angus Walker from Axmouth was originally opposed to the scheme, which forced him to sell his trawler and buy a smaller boat, under 10 m, like the other 41 boats operating from the four ports. He now acknowledges that the fish "are of better quality, the sole and plaice are fatter and in better condition and can fetch a higher price while lack of disturbance of the seabed is helping to sustain a healthy food chain. The captures of lobster and crab have also improved."

Present day worries about unsustainable overexploitation of marine resources are far from a new phenomenon. In *The Unnatural History of the Sea* Callum Roberts tells how, as early as 1376 a complaint was made to Edward III requesting that he should ban a new and destructive type of fishing gear, essentially a beam trawl.

The ban was needed as the trawl had destroyed the spawn of oysters and mussels as well as catching so many small fish that they had to be fed to fatten pigs. The commoners petitioning the king were well aware that the small fish were what the great fish needed to feed upon.

Beer Beach in 1964

Edible Crab - built for strength, not speed

Callum maintains that "in my work as a scientist I find that few people really appreciate how far the oceans have been altered from their pre-exploitative state."

He then tells of the loss of seals, whales and turtles as well as the huge populations of cod, sturgeon, tuna and herring and advocates a new approach to marine conservation.

Most governments now agree that we need more reserves and MPAs but emerging scientific understanding of human impacts suggests that marine reserves must be extensive to sustain ecological processes and services like fisheries that support humanity. Blue Marine agrees, aiming to increase the area of the oceans' water under protection to 10% by 2020 and 30% by 2030 and it maintains that "overfishing represents a major security issue and has devastating consequences for the fragile diversity of our planet."

PAST PRACTICE (2007)
with most areas open to exploitation

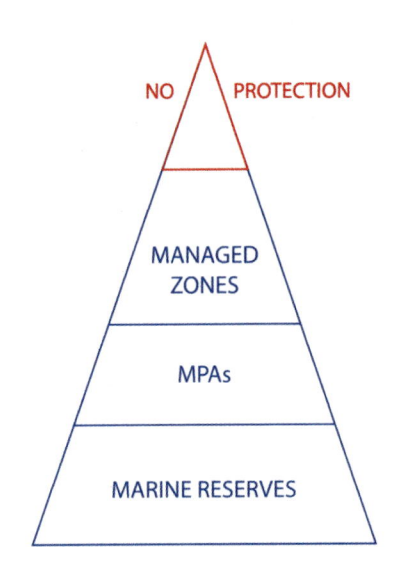

- Reserves and MPAs less than 1% of seas
- INTENSE EXPLOITATION AREA

A POTENTIAL FUTURE
marine reserves must be extensive

- NO PROTECTION
- MANAGED ZONES
- MPAs
- MARINE RESERVES

Rockpool life illustrated at Seaton Jurassic

This fragile diversity and the range of lifeforms in accessible rock pools is well displayed in Seaton Jurassic or at first hand in the pools below Whitecliff. If the tide is low and still going out and if you have the confidence to move safely over large, slippery rocks you can clamber along the beach from Beer to Seaton, rock pooling on the way. Dr Colin Dawes who produced illustrated accounts of many of our Jurassic Classic walks claimed that any small brown fish seen darting about the bottom of the pool was a "Biddlenob" or Tompot Blenny. On one walk we caught three of these fish which adapted their appearance to the colour of the dish they were in. He illustrated a fine Corkwing Wrasse with red and green stripes on its cheeks.

Another of his favourites was the Piddock or Rock Maggot, a bivalve mollusc which contrasts with the Honeycomb Worm, Sabellaria, in that the mollusc bores into soft rocks whereas the worm builds up tubes of sand, derived from the sandstone high in the cliffs, to form a crusty reef. Two special animals of these rock pools are Sea Hares, purple-brown slugs with ear-like appendages and Worm Pipefish which Colin described as "like a thick piece of discarded bootlace."

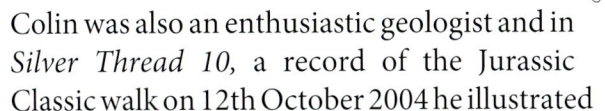

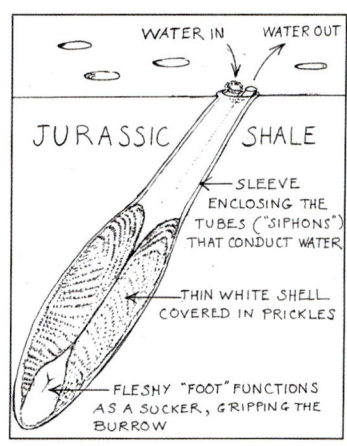

Colin was also an enthusiastic geologist and in *Silver Thread 10,* a record of the Jurassic Classic walk on 12th October 2004 he illustrated the features of the strata at Seaton Hole. At the base are the Whitecliff sandstones, which when undermined by the sea give rise to caves roofed with chert. Above that a distinctive band of Cenomanian Limestone and the hard white nodules of Middle Chalk with flint in bands above. He illustrated the Middle Chalk zone of Inoceramus labiatus with a drawing of this slipper-shaped seashell characterised by well-defined concentric ridges.

For most people it is easier to avoid the beach and follow the coast path from Beer. This descends to the Old Beer Road giving a fine view of the cliffs to the west of Seaton Hole and the possibility of refreshments or a steep descent to the beach and a low tide meander to Seaton.

Since part of the Old Beer Road collapsed in July 2012 a detour inland has been established. This is useful at high tide enabling you to reach Seaton by road, rather than along the beach. On your left you pass a bank with summer orchids and Nottingham Catchfly and continue on to Cliff Field. Here we have a splendid labyrinth, an informative timeline and a fine view of the coastal geology.

The Piddock or Rock Maggot

Sabellaria colony below the Undercliff

Seaton features prominently in the story of *Winefred* written by the prolific novelist and hymn writer Sabine Baring-Gould. The story appeared in serial form in 1899 and as a book a year later. In 2011 the Visitor Centre Trust supported "The Heritage Players" in a community play with the novel having been adapted for the stage by John Seward and Penny Elsom. The story starts in 1830s Seaton "a disregarded hamlet by the mouth of the Axe picking up a precarious existence by being visited by bathers in the summer". Long abandoned by her husband and having lost their cottage in a cliff fall, Jane and her 18-year-old daughter Winefred try to find work and accommodation in the town. They fail and trudge through the November rain along Seaton beach towards the ferry at Axmouth, run by the unscrupulous Olver Dench. "On the further side, the chalk with dusty sandstone underneath, rears itself into a bold headland."

At the top of this headland Jane, depressed, cold and wet tries to throw Winefred over the cliff edge but fails. When she recovers Winefred finds herself in a warm cottage belonging to Job Rattenbury, whose house "was cut off from the sea by a sheer face of the precipice."

Next day Job sends Winefred to Beer with a secret message for the smugglers there and for his son Jack. Later Winefred meets, but for obvious reasons doesn't recognise, her father Mr Holwood, on the beach east of the Axe. She also overhears plans to trap the smugglers. She then finds a new rift opening up as she climbs the precarious cliff. That evening she warns the smugglers about the trap and directs them to hide their barrels in the new rift where, after a rock fall, she gets trapped. Jack rescues her.

Later, after problems between Jane and Jack and diversions in Bath, the story ends with another highly eventful day. Job has a stroke after attacking Jane who had seen him opening a money-filled secret drawer. This gives Dench the chance to return and search the cottage, find the money and leave Jane bound and gagged. As he escapes a new chasm opens up. Dench overbalances, grabs a tuft of wiry grass and hawkweed but still goes down into the chasm.

Jane is rescued and reconciled with her husband. Jack, after almost killing himself on Whitecliff collecting Choughs for Jane, passionately embraces her and the story ends "what a day this has been for rending asunder and for joining together."

The 'bold headland' of Haven Cliff

The Chough - by the second half of the nineteenth century the species was almost extinct in Devon

'In a moment Winefred was in his arms and the cage and the birds had fallen'

> "There are other considerations involving the perpetual conflict between the idealists and the realists – those who would not have irreplaceable amenities destroyed forever and those who would sacrifice them to supply an immediate need." – WD Lang, expert on the Blue Lias, writing to Sir Arthur Tansley in response to the threat of conifer planting in 1949.

Winefred had struggled and escaped from her mother's grasp at the top of Haven Cliff. The cliffs themselves have had their escapes from the threat of a giant holiday camp, a tourist ropeway and extensive forestry. In 1939 Cornish Riviera Estates proposed a holiday camp for 500 people at Dowlands Farm but geologist Muriel Arber had better ideas when she wrote in *Country Life* that "In the hundred years that have passed since the landslip occurred some of the features of the Chasm have softened but the untouched wildness of the scene still presents a grand and inspiring spectacle. It is greatly to be hoped that these cliffs and undercliffs may be preserved from the exploitation with which they have been threatened."

Muriel hoped that the Undercliffs might be secured for the nation which is what happened in 1953 when the Nature Conservancy bought out the holiday camp owners. Their plans for Dowlands had been spoiled by the war. The Forestry Commission's plan for afforestation had also been thwarted but another threat was raised in the Axmouth Study of 1971 which suggested that the cliffs "at Axmouth command such magnificent views that the idea of a ropeway to take visitors up the eastern end of the gravel bank, over the Axe and on to the top of the cliff adjoining the golf course has been mooted. The economics of such a venture would be that a hundred thousand passengers would be needed to justify the running costs."

Since that time the problem for Haven Cliff has been the development of dense scrub which has made access difficult and greatly reduced the botanically rich south facing grassland. Good populations of Nottingham Catchfly still survive and in a couple of recent years the reserve's only Broadleaved Helleborine appeared. Butterflies and Adders love the warmth. Around the cliff face Fulmars, Ravens and Peregrines are often to be seen but a spectacular landslip in 2014 not only changed the landscape but made access even more difficult.

The untouched wildness of the scene

Phil Parr on Haven Cliff

Trees have softened the features of the Chasm

Ecology was a little-known science and knowledge of the biological interest of the undercliffs was limited when the Nature Conservancy was declared in 1949. Soon after that declaration L J Watson heard that there were plans to plant conifers on part of the landslip. He managed to visit immediately and his report on the 8th July started a flurry of correspondence. On 13th October Sir Arthur Tansley, pioneering plant ecologist and first chairman of the Conservancy, was asked to provide a letter giving a "strong scientific not amenity (I repeat not amenity) grounds for not proceeding with planting as now contemplated."

In the limited time available Tansley mobilised Cambridge opinion, including that of WJ Arkell FRS whose note was short and to the point. "These landslips are the largest and most instructive in the whole coast of England. The Dowlands Chasm and a great slipped mass in front are unique and should be kept free at all costs."

At the end of November the planting plans were sidelined for the time being but despite this, on 25th July 1950, a group led by Tansley met to inspect and consult. Observing from the top of the cliff above the Chasm, Forestry Commissioner, Sir William Taylor, thought that the instability of the ground and the scattered nature of the sheltered patches made the landslip unsuitable for forestry. In the afternoon the party met Major Allhusen, landowner and chairman of East Devon Planning Committee, together with planners and councillors in a beech plantation below Pinhay. At that meeting came the first suggestion that the stretch of coast fully merited being treated as a National Reserve.

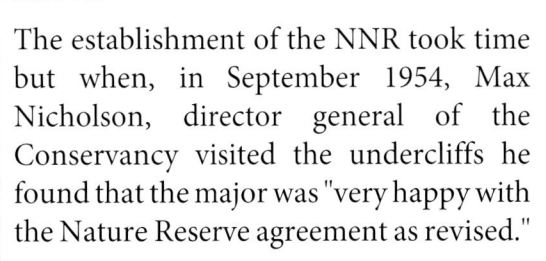

The establishment of the NNR took time but when, in September 1954, Max Nicholson, director general of the Conservancy visited the undercliffs he found that the major was "very happy with the Nature Reserve agreement as revised."

Most of the 305 ha of the National Nature Reserve was designated on 16th of March 1955 with Rousdon and Charton Cliffs being added on 17th July 1956.

The Chasm and Goat Island, 1968

The Nature Conservancy acquired the first National Nature Reserve, 4250 acres around Beinn Eighe for £3500 in November 1951

Sir Arthur Tansley near Corfe Castle in 1954

The 'Prow' and pillbox from across the Axe — JAMES HARRIS

Tiny Bog Pimpernel — MIKE LOCK

Marsh Helleborine also flowers on dry Goat Island — PETER VERNON

Pyramidal Orchids

The public footpath, much of it recently resurfaced to improve access to the fishermen's boats and Blue Marine storage centre, leads from the two bridges over the Axe towards the mouth of the river. There another new feature "The Prow", an eastern outlier of Seaton Jurassic, provides seating and views across the bay towards Beer Head. Behind it the 1940 concrete pillbox is the last or the first of a series of such structures which, along with concrete tank traps, are the remains of the Taunton Stop Line constructed when German invasion threatened. In August 2018 Seaton's 17th blue plaque for places of historic interest was attached to the pillbox. The remains of Hallett's pier are a reminder of the varied history of the harbour.

The walk from the mouth of the Axe to Culverhole is a hard slog over rounded pebbles and under Triassic rocks which drip with seepages, in one of which a rare cranefly was found. At the base of the cliff fallen material often accumulates. At low tide the red rocks show as ledges and in the rock pools are extensive mussel beds with their attendant Dog Whelk predators. There are also reefs of the Honeycomb Worm. Approaching Culverhole the pebbles change to larger grey "cow stones". The cliffs' colour also changes as they decrease in height and at the base of a low cliff is some distinctive White Lias rock.

Culverhole is typical "soft cliff" made up of collapsed chalk and greensand with bare areas and seepages. In the brief survey in July 2002 David Gibbs found seven nationally scarce invertebrates.

In *Wildflowers of the Devon Coast* David J Allen describes the wet, base rich habitat there as coastal fen. Here the handsome Marsh Helleborine flowers in July. Its purplish-brown and white flowers are adapted, as are many orchid flowers, to ensure pollination by bees. Earlier in the year Southern Marsh-orchids produce dense spikes of rose magenta, each with a broad flat lip that is spotted in the centre. A much rarer plant, Marsh Fragrant-orchid also grows here with Black Bog-rush, Great Horsetail and Bog Pimpernel; its fragrance is unusual among British orchids but is common among moth and butterfly pollinated flowers. The petals are deep pink to magenta and the three lobed lip has a very slender spur. This, writes David, separates it from all other British orchids except Pyramidal which grows on Goat Island, The Plateau and on the clifftop. Since the rerouting of the coast path, access to ever-changing Culverhole, with its special habitats and slightly chaotic features, is much less easy except from the beach.

Following botanical research in 2003 Michael Cooke described Culverhole as an "extensive section of landslip with continuous active slumping in many areas. Steep soft cliff dominated by silty sand with frequent loose stone and flint materials ranging from small fragments to boulder size. A further section of failed cliff lies upslope dominated by uneven exposed limestone outcrops and fallen limestone blocks and scree with areas of soft cliff dominated by sandy silt."

Collapsing Culverhole

The instability evident in 2003 became critical in 2014 when the arcuate backscar of the soft cliff began to move, taking the coastal path steps with it. District Council Ranger Dave Palmer found that steps he had replaced earlier in the year now needed further attention. As a consequence reserve manager Tom Sunderland brought together a group to consider the situation. It was evident that no steps would survive for long and as all alternative routes presented their own problems, he taped off the potentially dangerous area closing the path for the foreseeable future. The county highway authority responsible for rights of way, diverted the path inland through the Rousdon estate to Shapwick and on towards Ware and Lyme Regis.

Ware Cliffs had themselves been a problem in 2013 and in *Open Country* on BBC Radio 4, Tom described seeing a major fall onto Monmouth Beach which had repercussions back to the inland cliff west of Chimney Rock. On the same programme Elaine Franks, whose *Sketchbook of the Undercliffs* had been published in 1989, recalled how, before regular clearance work, she had almost stumbled into a bramble filled sheepwash.

In 2014, the route from the sheepwash to the beach was blocked and, following repeated storms and high tides, soft clays and large boulders, up to 8 m³ in volume, had collapsed, while the action of the sea had buried many of the best fossils at the slabs. To the west, at the base of Haven Cliff there was some erosion of lengths of Triassic rock but movement was mainly from above where Foxmould, weathered to soft loose sand, had fallen onto the beach.

Bridleway through the Rousdon Estate

Shapwick Viaduct carried the old Lyme Regis railway

Culverhole was among sites visited during a Bioblitz held on 30th July 2011 when 40 field naturalists, helped by local guides, searched likely localities to find as many species as possible in 24 hours.

Specialists also searched Goat Island, above Culverhole, both during the day, when a good range of chalk grassland flowers were found, and at night when moth enthusiasts set up light traps at the edge of the sea cliff. With some moths flying by day, and others attracted to lights elsewhere in the undercliffs, 252 species in all were identified. Also at night, Anabat detectors told Fiona Matthews more about the six bat species present than did the disappointing harp nets which caught nothing.

Martin Drake added greatly to knowledge of fly populations recording 186 species. Mark Pool identified 67 mosses and liverworts and Barbara Benfield 98 lichens and although both had worked in the undercliffs before, their lists included several new records for the reserve. Very few fungi were found, no expert mycologist was around, and only a few beetles. If we had had a specialist in coleoptera available the total of 1125 species on land could have risen to 1300. Additional species were found offshore by Devon Seasearch.

Yellow Meadow-ant nest, Lasius flavus

When all goes well the resulting grassland, with older areas characterised by "hills" created by Yellow Meadow-ants, hold a rich flora including many tiny plants like Autumn Ladies-tresses, Fairy Flax, Squinancywort and Wild Thyme which, like Rock Rose, favours the anthills. These are made up of smaller soil particles, have better drainage through the ants' galleries and a higher potassium level than surrounding areas.

Goat Island is a key site historically and biologically and over recent years Natural England, together with volunteers, has increased the level of management, not only maintaining the existing grassland but also clearing scrub and trees from areas which, as shown by aerial photographs, had been grassland in the 1950s. With no water to support or fences to restrain grazing animals, whether goats or not, management involves the use of machine scythes and brush cutters to clear woody vegetation, nettles, thistles and the more aggressive grasses. Raking off the cut material to reduce fertility is a vital follow-up process.

Botanising on Goat Island

Triggerfish, one of the many additional species found by Devon Seasearch

Goat Island and the Chasm contrast with intensively farmed land

In the 19th century the clifftop path from Dowlands leading into the undercliffs was often known as the Goat's Path. This may explain the name Goat Island which is an island only in the sense that its sides are steep, with screes, ridges and pinnacles resulting from the 1839 landslip and subsequent erosion. In the landslip the great mass of chalk, on which corn and turnips had been growing, slid forward overnight leaving a great sunken chasm between it and the mainland.

Much research and discussion has centred around the mechanism of the landslip but a paper by Ramues Gallois in 2010 maintained that the description by the Reverends Buckland and Conybeare together with surveyor William Dawson is superior to that of any subsequent account. His paper's subtitle "almost right first time" shows his belief that the original description is the best and "an outstanding example of observation and analysis". His summary of the mechanisms seem simple enough. "The whole mass (Goat Island) then moved forward over the fluidised sand and pushed the terraces of debris that had been formed by earlier landslides forward, to create a new cliff line. At the seaward edge, the Cretaceous debris that had formed the old sea cliff was pushed across underlying Triassic and Jurassic rocks to form offshore reefs."

Richard Edmonds however remains unsatisfied with this explanation and with the detail and orientation of Conybeare's famous sectional drawing though part of the landslip area. Richard suggests that Goat Island moved south and east as well as rotating slightly to widen the eastern end of the Chasm. This movement was perhaps triggered by the reactivation of the old Dowlands and Plateau slips following heavy rain and marine erosion. He used drone surveys and persistent footwork to record details of the remote ridges south-east of Goat Island. He also believes that the beaches below the sheepwash and plateau provide critical evidence of the reactivation of the two older slips.

Squinancywort, a herb for sore throats

The ruins occasioned by the earthquake or landslip

Autumn Gentian - up to 30,000 can be sen on Goat Island

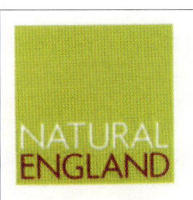

Between 2006 and 2009 Ramues Gallois wrote three reports for Natural England on the geology of The Undercliffs. The cover shows the reaping of the corn and inside he describes how 'fields sown with winter corn remained intact on a detached slab and were ceremoniously harvested the following autumn by nubile virgins wielding large scythes, amid scenes of joyous celebration.'

The 2007 report includes an illustration showing Chasm Cliff a few days after the landslip. Artist Mary Buckland painted three members of the Upper Greensand, a seepage line in the Foxmould and a gully in the cliff which exposes more details of nine strata measured by Ramues on site.

Chasm Cliff, a watercolour by Mary Buckland, December 1839

Figure 17. Watercolour by Mary Buckland showing the back face (Chasm Cliff) of the 1839 Bindon Landslip a few months after the event. The members of the Upper Greensand can be clearly distinguished. Note the seepage line at the base of the oxidised Whitecliff Chert Member. The gully referred to in Figure 13 is probably that arrowed here.

The reaping of the corn

"Above the sea of foliage the white cliffs shoot out in the boldest fashion and out of the gorge start horns, pinnacles of chalk, of the most fantastic desolation." – Sabine Baring-Gould writing in December 1898.

made off to the cliff edge tipping his rider into the chasm. At one time described as "too much like a gravel pit", the chasm initially had few trees but since 1900 it has developed, to the fascination of ecologists, into a truly natural Ash/Field Maple woodland which, unlike much of the undercliffs is free from exotic invaders like Holm Oak. Now many of the trees are at risk from Ash Die Back disease which has now arrived in the Undercliff.

At the west end of the Chasm is an old Devon bank, a field boundary that subsided some 200 feet along with the wheat and turnip fields and an orchard. On 14th August 1840 the reaping of the corn was celebrated as William Dawson described in a note to Prof Buckland. "It was a really beautiful sight – the day warm and bright – and I should think a full 6000 spectators. They got up a procession which was, in my humble opinion, not quite in good taste – a committee with blue ribands around the neck – six lady reapers in white kid gloves and wreaths of artificial flowers, the sickles tied with blue, and six gentlemen to match in blue vests and white trousers. They had however, a good band of music, the effect as they wound down the zig-zag path into the valley of the chasm with the banners and assembled thousands lining the cliffs was picturesque and fine. Sir W Pole was there and furnished a battery of guns."

A fortnight later, as crowds gathered for the arrival of Queen Victoria from Torquay, a fine young merchant from Holland fell to his death when his horse

The Chasm, with Goat Island on the right, ca. 1905

A ridge from the east end of the chasm is sometimes followed on one of Natural England's undercliff walks. In March the woodland is full of wild daffodils and the ridge leads, somewhat indirectly, through them and on towards the coast path and a large Sheepwash. This was built between 1790 and 1800. Early maps still showed the area as pasture but as grazing reduced, trees took over. By the late 1980s, when Norman Barns and Terry Sweeney started clearance and restoration, the Sheepwash was almost entirely hidden. But now, following further work by Natural England, there is easy access. When in use shepherds led their sheep down the slope into a large sunken bath where the animals were rubbed down with Fuller's Earth to get rid of the grease and then with lime to whiten the fleece and increase its value.

The water supply, now dried up, also supplied nearby Landslip Cottage which had been built with stone from properties destroyed in 1839. The cottage is often associated with Annie Gapper who provided teas there until the 1950s. Much earlier her mother had done the same and in 1907 a Mr HM Fewens wrote in the visitors' book that "we, the undersigned, certify that in all Devonshire is no place like the landslip, no air so fresh, no tea like Mrs Gapper's."

A mile further east a route leaves the coast path and leads to an area of chalk grassland, the Plateau. A few thousand years ago this huge block of chalk became detached from the inland cliff and descended to its present position. Although the grassland community, like that of Goat Island, is now regularly mown its plant life, like its history, is different. Harebells, very rare in Devon, occur here while the anthills, with their distinctive soil structure, drainage and chemistry, are covered in Rock Roses. In some years the tiny, very rare annual, the Spring Gentian, appears on the cliff edge.

The Sheepwash

Landslip Cottage — CHARLES GROVER

Cliff at the east end of the Chasm

From the Sheepwash a somewhat obscure path leads down to the beach where, as the tide goes out, the remains of a Brixham trawler and a digger, optimistically driven from Seaton, are conspicuous among the rocks. A little further east, the falling tide also reveals the fossil rich slabs of Blue Lias limestone. These are similar to rocks west of Lyme but here the beds labelled 45 and 43 by WD Laing in his meticulous study of the strata in the cliffs above Pinhay Bay, are on the beach at The Slabs.

In 2014, winter storms which three times exceeded the theoretical once in 50 years threshold, led to more cliff erosion in Dorset than in Devon, but rain and high tide was sufficient to lead to a spectacular landslide on Haven Cliff. Huge Greensand blocks and debris fell from the clifftop while lower down, weathered rock subsided four or five metres pouring sodden material and trees over the edge and onto the beach.

The storms also led to subsidence above Culverhole which led Tom Sunderland to plan an alternative line for the coast path. An attempt to open a way through dense scrub near the south facing base of Goat Island failed while the steep and unstable terrain between the Chasm and the Sheepwash was deemed unsuitable, so a line of steps from Goat Island to the surviving coast path was created in anticipation of the path which eventually materialised.

View of the Haven Cliff landslide, May 2014

Coroniceras, an early Jurassic ammonite

The Jurassic nautiloid Cenoceras at the Slabs

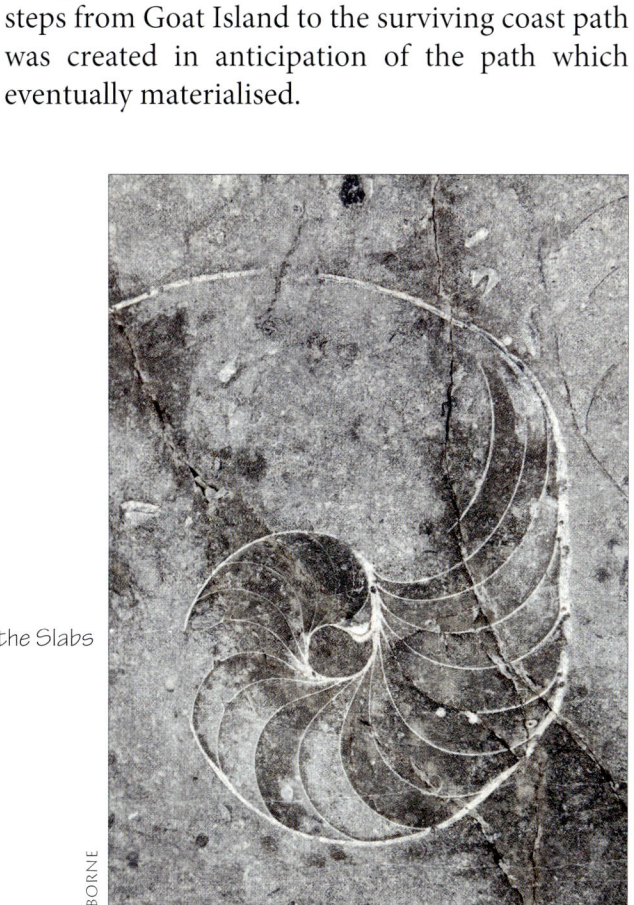

RECENT DEVELOPMENTS

Throughout the year significant projects continued. The building of Seaton Jurassic had begun in 2014 but now internal installations were taking shape with a skilled team creating the "Time Travellers" library, arranged to explain local landslips and geological strata, and the "Time Ship" ready to explore the distant past and its marine life. Next door the cliffs and rock pools at Seaton Hole were being constructed while outside the "Infinity Pool", showing sea life in Lyme Bay still needed more work.

In October the local *View From* newspaper quoted Councillor Ian Skinner who spoke of "positive partnerships" and of how the District Council were making good use of its land to bring huge economic and regeneration benefits to Seaton. The Council contributed £1.9 million to Seaton Jurassic and other major supporters included the County Council, the Heritage Lottery Fund and the Coastal Communities Forum. The Town Council and charitable foundations also made significant contributions. Volunteers planted out the wildlife garden and continue to be active in the wetlands. There, a new information centre "The Lookout" had opened near the reserve entrance, on the cycle route past Black Hole Marsh.

This development of the Stop Line Way cycle route was important in two ways, for its progress through the reserve and into Colyford gave promise that it would eventually achieve its goal of crossing the whole of the south-west peninsula to Minehead. It also meant that with a new all-weather surface, disabled visitors, using their own transport or the on-site Tramper, could reach all parts of the reserve. Once past the Discovery Hut and the Reed Base education centre they could cross an elaborate new bridge over the Stafford Brook before going on to Colyford Common. The tram company shared their ambition with plans for a new station in Seaton where three trams could be based and the risk of the line being flooded could be reduced.

By April 2016 Seaton Jurassic was ready for opening and, perhaps unusually, this happened three times. First Dr Iain Stewart, geologist and television presenter, was the keynote speaker. Two days later the public had their first chance to visit. Finally, in April the Princess Royal arrived by helicopter for the main celebration.

In the same month the coast path through the undercliffs reopened after the County Council had negotiated the route along the edge of the Bindon estate and into the National Nature Reserve. There Natural England had selected a way across Goat Island and down through woodland to join the existing path. The solid steps needed, involved some heavy carrying!

The 'Time Ship' begins to take shape

The Princess Royal unveils the plaque

Changes, such as those of 2015, are nothing new but, given sufficient time, their extent is almost incomprehensible. Between 250 and 200 mya, or million years ago, the red Triassic rocks, now at the base of Haven Cliff, east of Seaton, and more extensively to the west, formed in desert conditions when "East Devon" was only a few degrees north of the equator. Later, in round terms between 200 and 150 mya, Jurassic rocks formed under marine conditions. Later the early Cretaceous Greensand, often rust coloured with iron compounds, accumulated in shallow seas. Some 100 mya rocks from these three geological periods were tilted to the East and erosion levelled off their surface.

After this the Gault, a very sticky blue-black clay which was deposited patchily, as a shallow sea invaded much of what is now south-west England. In *The Hidden Landscape* Richard Fortey wrote "that the Gault is unreliable stuff, it engenders landslips when it is loaded with water as it does west of Lyme Regis, in Folkestone and in several sites on the Isle of Wight."

The Upper Greensand, only green when freshly exposed, contains fossil bivalves, gastropods and echinoids. These can be found in fallen blocks on the beach. Above it is the Chalk, so characteristic of Beer, formed as tiny algal coccoliths fell to the bottom and gradually accumulated. In his notes for a walk around Beer, Jurassic coast ambassador Mike Green tells how the village site was lifted above sea level some 25 mya by which time Devon was about 40° north and the Atlantic Ocean was beginning to form.

Over the last two million years a series of ice ages have seen sea levels rise and fall with Lyme Bay dry at the time of maximum ice 18,000 years ago and flooded as ice melted 8,000 years later.

The Winchester eco-archaeologists investigated change around the Axe over the last 5,000 years and the boundary hedge between Seaton and Colyton has been there for 1,000 years. On the beach near the "Slabs" parts of a Brixham trawler, the *Farway*, which ran aground in 1978 are rusting away after less than 40 years, as is a digger, optimistically driven from Seaton on a salvage mission.

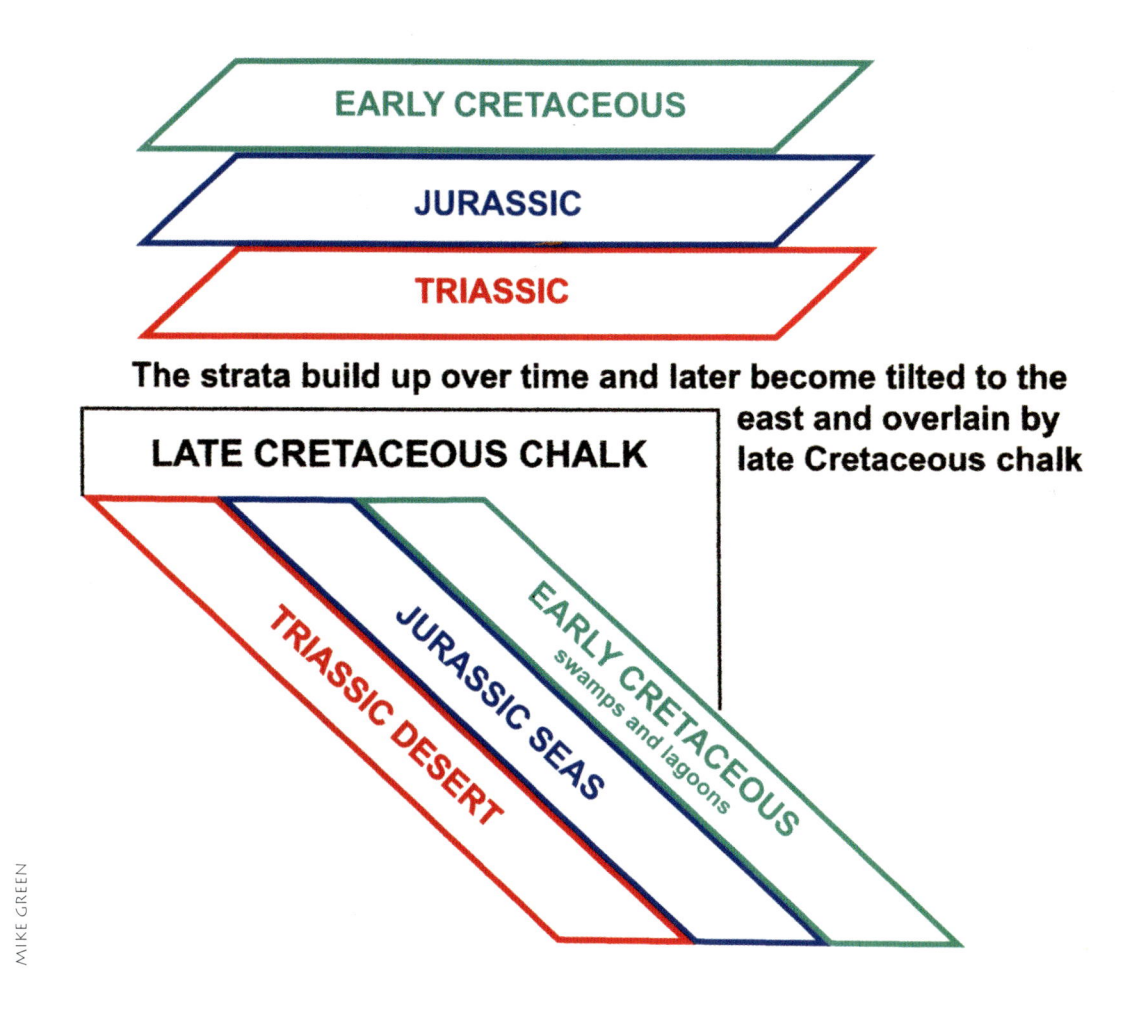

MIKE GREEN

Mike Green's model of the development of the Jurassic Coast

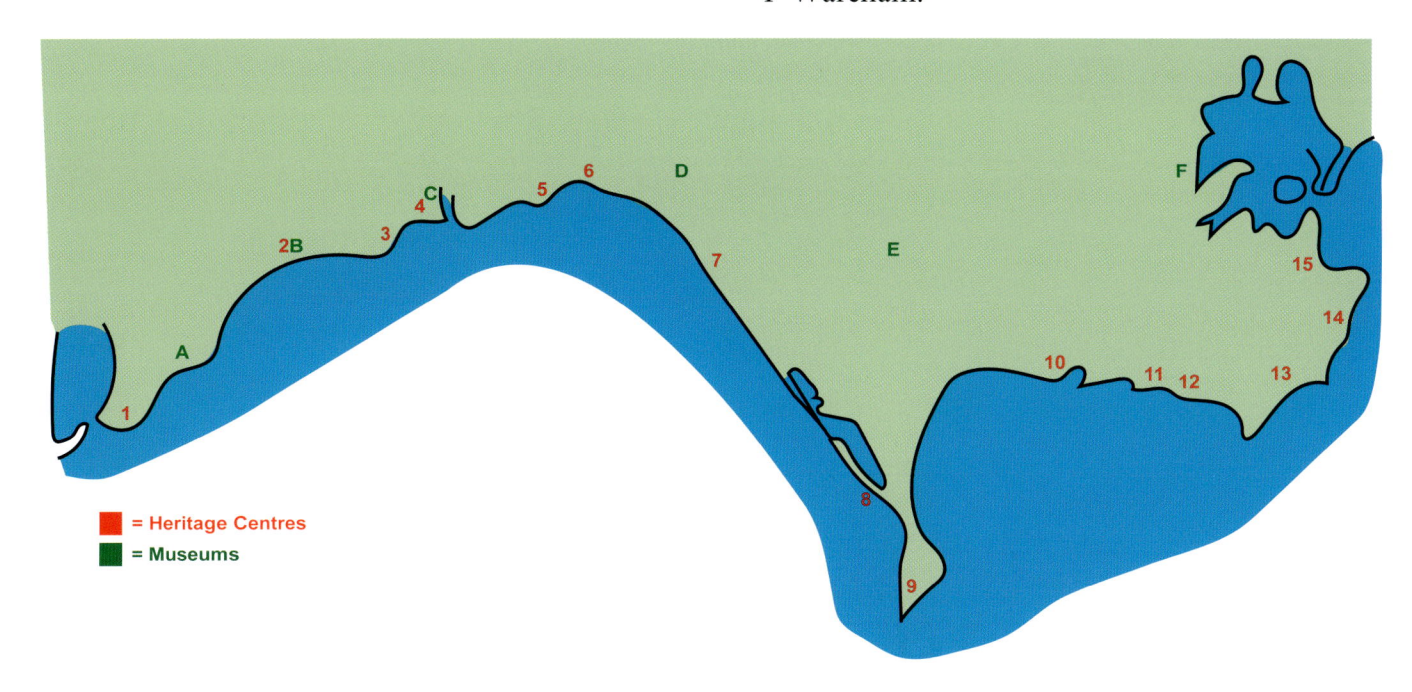

Where next? Most of these centres, listed from west to east, have been established since 2000

1 Orcombe Point Geoneedle, Exmouth
2 The Arches Centre, Sidmouth
3 Fine Foundation Centre, Beer.
4 Seaton Jurassic (Devon Wildlife Trust).
5 Lyme Regis Shelters and Philpot Museum.
6 Heritage Coast Centre, Charmouth.
7 West Bay Discovery Centre.
8 Fine Foundation Chesil Beach Centre.
9 Portland Bill Visitor Centre.
10 Lulworth Cove Heritage Centre.
11 Fine Foundation Centre, Kimmeridge.
12 Etches Collection, Kimmeridge.

13 Durlstone Castle Visitor Centre and National Nature Reserve.
14 Swanage Museum and Heritage Centre.
15 Studland Bay Discovery Centre.

The **museums** with many differences in scale and age include those at

A-Budleigh Salterton
B-Sidmouth
C-Seaton
D-Bridport
E-Dorchester
F-Wareham.

= Heritage Centres
= Museums

WEBSITES OF COUNTRYSIDE SERVICE PARTNERS

Axe Estuary Ringing Group www.axeestuaryringinggroup.blogspot.co.uk

Axe Vale and District Conservation Society www.axevaleconservation.org.uk

Beer Village Heritage Centre www.beervillageheritage.org.uk

Devon Wildlife Trust www.devonwildlifetrust.org

East Devon AONB www.eastdevonaonb.org.uk

National Trust www.nationaltrust.org.uk/southwest

Natural England www.naturalengland.org.uk

Seaton Jurassic www.seatonjurassic.org

Seaton Visitor Centre Trust www.seatonvisitorcentretrust.org

Seaton Tramway www.tram.co.uk

Other websites include

Axe Valley Heritage Museum www.seatonmuseum.co.uk

Beer Quarry Caves www.beerquarrycaves.co.uk

Buglife www.buglife.org.uk

Bus Times www.travelinesw.com

Cycling www.sustrans.org.uk

JC World Heritage Site www.jurassiccoast.org

South West Coast Path www.southwestcoastpath.com

South West MCZs https://tinyurl.com/AxeMCZ

Seasearch www.seasearch.org.uk

An early programme for Autumn/Winter 2014/15

SELECTED BIBLIOGRAPHY

Allen, DJ (2000) *Wildflowers of the East Devon Coast.*

Axe Bird Group (2006-2010) *Axe Estuary and Seaton Bay Bird Reports.*

Axe Estuary Ringing Group (2018) *The First 10 Years 2007-2016.*

Axe Vale and District Conservation Society (1980-2018) *Newsletters.*

Axminster Rural and Seaton Urban District Councils (1970) *The Axmouth Study.*

Baring-Gould, S (1900) *Winefred, a Story of the Chalk Cliffs.*

Berry, L & Gosling, G (1996) *The Book of the Axe.*

Brunsden, D (Ed.) (2003) *The Official Guide to the Jurassic Coast.*

Butler, J (Ed.) (2000) *Travels in Victorian Devon.* (Peter Orlando Hutchinson).

Conybeare, WD, Buckland, W., & Dawson, W (1840) *Ten plates.*

Crowe, I (2001) *Seaton Marshes Second Management Plan.*

Dawes, C (2006) *Rock pooling around Lyme Regis*

Day, O (2018) *The Lyme Bay Marine Reserve.* (In the Marshwood no. 233).

Edwards, RA & Gallois, RW (2004) *The Geology of Sidmouth and District.*

Gallois, RW (2010) *The Failure Mechanism of the 1839 Bindon Landslide.*

Gosling, T & Clement, M (2008) *Axmouth Village.*

Gray, T (Ed.) (1998) *Travels in Georgian Devon* (The Rev. John Swete).

Henwood, B (2012) *Branscombe 1930.* In Devon Newsletter 83 of Butterfly Conservation.

Lousley, JE (1950) *Wildflowers of Chalk and Limestone.*

Naylor, P (2011) *Great British Marine Animals.* 3rd edition.

Parkinson, M (1985) *The Axe Estuary and its Marshes.* Devonshire Association 117.

Prater, AJ (1981) *Estuary Birds.*

Proctor, M (2013) *Vegetation of Britain and Ireland.*

Pulman, G (1875) *The Book of the Axe.* 4th edition.

Roberts, C (2007) *The Unnatural History of the Sea.*

Rees, SE et al. (2015) *The Socio-Economic Effects of a Marine Protected Area.*

Scott, J & Gray, C (2004) *Out of Darkness.* (Beer Quarry Caves).

Seaton Development Trust (2003) *Seaton and the Axe Valley.*

Sheehan, EV et al. (2013) *Recovery of a Temperate Reef Assemblage in an MPA.*

Smallshire, D & Swash, A (2010) *Britain's Dragonflies.* 2nd edition.

Steers, JA (1953) *The Sea Coast.*

Turton, SD & Weddell, PJ (1993) *Archaeological Appraisal of the Salt Industry.*

Walters, D (2004-2006) *Axe Estuary Bird Reports.*

Whitehouse, A (2007) *Managing Soft Cliffs for Invertebrates.*

Wilkinson, K et al. (2006) *Axe Estuary Wetlands; a Geo- and Bio-archaeological Assessment.*

Woolmoor, R (2009) *East Devon AONB: a Designation History.*

78 TRAVEL AROUND THE AXE

Regular tram trips run from March to October but only for special events at other times

GILL CROWE

Some hazards in and below the Undercliffs

TOM SUNDERLAND, NATURAL ENGLAND

A well-fed tick

COLIN WEST

Protect yourself against parasitic ticks which can be numerous, or large when well fed

Stuart Line Cruises sometimes come to Seaton, sailing on to Lyme Regis or back towards Branscombe

Ticks on Stinking Iris next to the coast path

TOM SUNDERLAND, NATURAL ENGLAND

ACKNOWLEDGEMENTS

The Axe Vale and District Conservation Society has worked with members of the District Council since Geoff Jones was Rural Affairs Officer and Nic Butler had a similar role with the East Devon Heritage Coast. When Fraser Rush was appointed and the Wetlands began to be developed, links between the Society and the Council's Countryside Service became even closer. More recently Devon Wildlife Trust have become much involved whether in the context of the marine life in Lyme Bay or in developing Seaton Jurassic.

Others who have helped the book on its way include David Walters who converted the original handwritten draft into a legible form that could be read by Prof Denys Brunsden, Dr Mike Lock and Fraser Rush. Their critical comments greatly improved the text. Ramues Gallois (Geology), Ted Gosling (Seaton history), John Scott (Beer Quarry Caves) and Tom Sunderland (Undercliff) have commented on their particular areas of expertise. The much changed text was brought to order again by Miriam Thomas while many of the illustrations were helped on their way by Dolph Zubic. The author is grateful to Creative Solutions of Axminster for their diagrams and maps, produced from his sketches. Among photographers Ben Osborne is thanked for his specially taken pictures, and thanks also go to Paul Naylor for his wonderful images of marine life and to Dave Smallshire for dragonflies and damsels. As a lifelong bird man I am grateful to Tim White, Steve Waite and others for a fine array of species from the Wetlands.

When Fraser Rush left the Countryside Service after 13 years of creative work it was a significant punctuation mark in the development of the wetlands. Reorganisation, following pressure on budgets, led to the creation of two team leader posts. Steve Edmonds, replaced by James Chubb in summer 2016, became the "Place" leader and therefore Wetlands manager. Tim Dafforn was appointed as "People" leader. Apart from the Wetlands the service manages ten Local Nature Reserves and runs an environmental service based on the Education Centre in the Wetlands. This offers sessions such as rock pooling and woodland activities at the Council's Reserves.

Thanks to those who lead the work in the Wetlands, the Undercliff, the AONB and along the Jurassic Coast, to the councillors at various levels who make critical decisions, and above all to the many volunteers who put so many hours into the conservation of this wonderful area.

Additional thanks to those associated with Lyme Regis Philpot Museum.

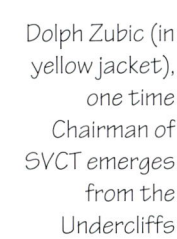

Nigel Burnell (in the front digger) and Richard Cadwgan (in the rear digger) during construction of the boardwalk to the island hide at Black Hole Marsh.

As well as the help of all those mentioned opposite, this book would never have emerged so attractively without the design skills and patience of John Marriage. He has, in the author's opinion, created an unusual visual delight.

Dolph Zubic (in yellow jacket), one time Chairman of SVCT emerges from the Undercliffs

James Chubb

ALLUVIUM. Deposits, such as sand and gravel, laid down by modern rivers.

ANABAT DETECTOR. The trade name for a particular type of bat detector which makes digital recordings of all sonic calls which can then be analysed to see which species have flown past.

ANTICLINE. A rock exposure in which the strata are folded upwards to form a convex dome.

BEAM TRAWL. Fish are caught in this large bag or net which is held open by wooden beam, managed by a single boat.

BELVEDERE. A raised turret or lantern erected on an eminence and used to view the surrounding area.

CHERT. Hard silica rock similar to flint.

COCCOLITHS. The ultimate components of chalk. These minute symmetrical rosettes of calcite are secreted by algae. Because of their size they are photographed by an electron microscope.

COW STONES. These are large boulders found on the beach and in the Foxmould of the Upper Greensand.

CRETACEOUS. The geological period, 145-66 million years ago, that followed the Jurassic. Dinosaurs and ammonites disappeared towards the end of the period.

EX SITU. Rocks or other deposits, which have been displaced from their original location.

ECHINOIDS. These form a class within the phylum Echinoderma: Sea Urchins

FILA. A filament or tenuous threadlike structure.

FOXMOULD. Soft greenish-grey sandstone weathering to a fox-coloured brown sand. When saturated it is unstable and this can lead to landslips.

FREESTONE. This is limestone that can be cut in any direction as found in Beer Quarry Caves.

GASTROPODS. Snails. The class of mollusc with a spiral shell.

GLAUCONITE. A hydrous silicate of iron, potassium or other base, commonly known as green earth.

GREENSAND. Sands containing glauconite have a greenish colour when first exposed.

HALOSERE. The series of plant communities tolerating different exposures to salt water as in an estuary or saltmarsh.

JURASSIC. The geological period 201-145 million years ago.

JURASSIC LIMESTONE. The Blue Lias made up of alternating layers of limestone and shale. The classic site is Pinhay Bay and the nearest to Seaton is slightly west of Culverhole.

MESOZOIC. Local rocks date from this era consisting of the Triassic, Jurassic, and Cretaceous periods.

MUDSTONE. Rock formed from consolidated clay but without the fine bedding of shale.

NEOLITHIC. The new stone age starting some 5000 years ago.

PANGAEA. The Triassic supercontinent composed of all today's continents, with its centre made up largely of deserts.

PERIOD. A unit of time, such as the Jurassic, during which rocks of a certain type formed.

QUATERNARY. The most recent period covering the last two million years.

QUOINS. The cornerstones of a wall or building.

RADIOCARBON DATING. The method of using the concentration of fast decaying carbon-14 to date comparatively recent organic remains such as bone or wood from the last 70,000 years.

S.A.C. A special area of conservation designated under the European Habitats Directive.

SANDSTONE. A sedimentary rock made up of cemented sand-sized particles.

SEDIMENTARY ROCKS. These were laid down as sediments usually by water but also by wind or ice.

SHEEPWASH. Sunken construction into which sheep could be directed to be degreased and whitened to increase the value of their wool.

SOFT CLIFFS. These are easily eroded leading to bare ground colonised by pioneer vegetation, habitats which support a rich diversity of invertebrates including rare and specialised species.

SYNCLINE. A downward fold in the rocks so the beds dip towards the centre.

TRIASSIC. The geological period at the start of the Mesozoic, 252-201 million years ago. Much of the East Devon Coast is characterised by these red rocks.

UNCONFORMITY. A considerable break in continuity and time so that two rock formations, e.g. Triassic and Cretaceous, are brought into contact despite their very different ages.

UNIFORMITARIANS. In contrast to catastrophists, they believe that even deep river valleys, like that of the Axe, were formed by normal forces acting over long periods of time, rather than by huge and sudden events like Noah's flood.

WHITE LIAS. A pale limestone layer now called the Langport member. Found at the base of cliffs west of Lyme and, less conspicuously, as the westernmost Jurassic rock in the cliff on the Seaton side of Culverhole.

INDEX

This index includes geological features, taxonomic groups, major locations and relevant organisations. A blue page number indicates an illustration.

Adders 61

Area of Outstanding Natural Beauty (AONB) 3, 28-30

Axe 3, 4, 6, 7, 13, 14-16, 20, 21, 23, 24, 25, 27-29, 40-45, 60, 64, 73, 77

Axe estuary ringing group 43-46, 77

Experts from Buglife during the Bioblitz

Axmouth 4, 10, 12, 15, 16, 19, 20-24, 34, 48, 54, 55, 57, 58, 60, 61, 64, 77

Axe Vale Conservation Society (AVDCS) 24, 28, 32, 34, 49, 76, 77, 82

Axe Yacht Club 23

Beer 3-5, 11, 15, 17, 18, 29, 37, 53, 54, 57-60, 64, 75

Bio-Archaeological survey of the marshes 14, 77

Bioblitz 41, 66

Birds, rare 36, 37

Bird reports 3, 36, 37, 43-46, 77

Birds at sea 32

Birds in the Underclifts 36, 61

Birds in the Wetlands 31, 37-39, 41-47

Black Hole Marsh 3, 24, 42, 72

Blue Lias 12, 61, 71, 81

Blue Marine Foundation 22, 54, 57, 58, 64

Borrow Pit 25, 31, 34

Bruckland Valley and Lakes 4, 25, 27

Buglife 52

Butterflies 50, 61, 77

Chalk 3, 5-7, 12, 13, 50, 52, 59, 64, 68, 77

Charmouth 9, 75

Chasm 16, 60-63, 67-71

Chert 6, 59, 60, 80

Chesil Bank 8, 9, 75

Chough 60

Clay with flints 5, 6, 52, 65

Clinton Devon Estates 19

Coly 3, 6, 14, 27, 29

Colyford Common/Marsh 3, 5, 6, 13, 14, 15, 36, 37, 44, 46, 47, 72

Colyton 3, 4, 6, 15, 17, 25, 78

Countryfile (TV) 46

Combpyne, in the East Devon AONB

INDEX

Countryside and Rights of Way Act 29

Cretaceous 7, 12, 50, 51, 67, 80

Culverhole 12, 55, 64, 65, 66, 71

Damselflies 26, 27

Devon Birdwatching and Preservation Society 37, 49

Devon County Council 49, 72

Devon Wildlife Trust 10, 18, 34, 55, 75

Devon Wildlife Trust and marine life 32, 33, 55

Dragonflies 26, 27, 31, 77, 83

East Devon AONB 2, 3, 18, 28, 29, 30, 49, 77

EDDC Countryside Service 9, 10, 28, 34, 37, 49, 63, 72, 82

East Devon Heritage Coast 25, 29, 30, 50, 53, 75

East Devon Way 3, 4

English Nature *see Natural England*

Enterprise Neptune 28

Environment Agency 37, 40, 49

Fine Family Foundation 10, 53, 75

Fossils 9, 71, 73

Goat Island 4, 5, 7, 63, 66, 67, 71, 72

Greater Horseshoe Bats 18

Greensand 5, 6, 12, 13, 64, 71, 80

Haven Cliff 7, 12, 14, 19, 60, 61, 71

Heritage Lottery Fund 19, 72

Holyford Woods 2, 4, 15, 28, 30, 34, 49

Hooken Undercliff 13, 50, 51

Invertebrates 25-27, 31, 32, 33, 37-39, 41, 47, 50, 52, 55-59, 61, 64-66, 73, 78

Jurassic Coast Trust 10, 53

Jurassic limestone/rocks 67, 80

Jurassic / World Heritage Coast 3, 5, 8, 9, 12, 13, 52-54, 77-78

Lyme Regis and part of the Dorset World Heritage Coast

BRIAN MARRIAGE

Male Banded Demoiselle, a striking damselfly

DAVE SMALLSHIRE

INDEX

Rock stacks at Ladram Bay
JOHN MARRIAGE

Ladram Bay 9

Ladybird, 13-spot 41

Landslip Cottage 70

Limestone 52, 53, 59, 65

Local Nature Reserves 14, 23, 28, 30, 31, 34, 37, 40, 41, 47, 49, 83

Lyme Bay 12, 32, 33, 55, 57, 72, 73, 77

Lyme Regis 6, 9, 58, 65, 71, 73, 75, 84

Marine and Coastal Access Bill 28, 33, 56

Marine Conservation Zones (MCZs) 33, 56

Marine mammals 32, 33, 58

Marine Protected Areas (MPAs) 33, 56, 57, 77

Mesozoic 80

Monmouth Beach 65

Moridunum 16

Mudstone 5-7, 12, 53

Natural England / English Nature 31, 34, 40, 49, 66, 68, 70, 72

National Trust 2, 8

Nature Conservancy Council 25, 63

National Parks 28, 30

Nautiloid 71

Odonata *see dragonflies*

Orcombe Point 9, 75

Otter 47

Peak Cliff 28

Philpot Museum 75, 84

Pinhay 12, 52, 63, 71

Plants 14, 38, 47, 48, 50, 53, 59, 61, 64, 66, 67, 70, 77

Plateau 5, 67, 70

Plymouth Marine Institute 57

Porpoise 32

Portland 75

Princess Royal 72

Radiocarbon dating 14

Rousdon 6, 65

Ruby Red cattle 31

Salt 16

The Geoneedle at Orcombe Point takes shape

INDEX

Sandstone 12, 59, 68, 81

Seaton 2, 5, 7, 10, 15, 16, 20, 21-23, 35, 59, 60, 64, 71-73, 75, 77, 78

Seaton Development Trust 9, 13, 25

Seaton Hole 4, 7, 10, 12, 34, 35, 59, 72

Seaton Jurassic / Discovery Centre 2, 4, 8, 28, 49, 59, 64, 72, 75

Seaton Town Council 23, 25

Seaton Visitor Centre Trust 19, 60

Seaton Wetlands 4, 9, 24, 25, 28, 30, 34, 40, 41

Self-regulating tide gate 37, 40

Sheepwash 65, 70, 81

Sidmouth 6, 75

Slabs, The 65, 71, 73

Soft cliffs 52, 64, 65, 77

Southwest Coast Path 76

Southwest Water 25, 34

Special Area of Conservation (SAC) 52

Stafford Brook 25, 30, 49

Stedcombe House 4, 15, 19

Stepps House 19

Swanage 75

Tram 4, 40, 44, 78

Triassic 3, 6, 7, 64, 65, 73, 80

Trinity Hill LNR 30

Undercliffs / The Landslip 2-4, 5, 10, 16, 28, 29, 34, 36, 52, 60-63, 65, 67-69, 70, 71, 78

Underhooken at Beer 4, 51, 85

Warners Holiday Camp 23

West Bay 58, 75

Wetland Bird Survey (WeBS) 36

Whitecliff 7, 10, 20, 22, 59

Winchester Cathedral 17

World Heritage Coast, *see Jurassic Coast*

A distinctive ash tree in the Underhooken

JOHN MARRIAGE

Snipe are among the hardest birds to count in the wetlands

COLIN VARNDELL

Durdle Door, a classic site on t Dorset Coast

SAM ROSE

Seaton "Between high Mountainous hills has a shelter'd situation, and the environs in point of picturesque beauty and varied rides are equal if not superior to most of the coast." - The Rev John Swete (1795) quoted in *Travels in Georgian Devon* (1998).

"The town deserves respect for it fighting qualities. Its battle has ever been a long one. The odds have been so tremendous. To go back to Leland in about 1540 it was "a mere fischer town" which had been far larger when the haven was good" - Francis Bickley in *Where Dorset meets Devon* (1911).